COMING ALIVE

A positive, affirmative guide to inner and outer health that combines the best features of leading contemporary self-development systems.

COMING ALIVE

A Practical Manual for Inner and Outer Health

by

Louis Proto

Illustrated by Mario Fournier

THORSONS PUBLISHING GROUP
Wellingborough, Northamptonshire

First published 1983
Second Edition 1987

© LOUIS PROTO 1987

British Library Cataloguing in Publication Data

Proto, Louis
The feeling good book: a practical manual
for inner and outer health. — 2nd ed.
1. Self-realisation
I. Title   II. Anand, Samarpan, *Swami*
Feeling good book
158'.1   BF637.S4

ISBN 0-7225-1439-5

*Published by Thorsons Publishers Limited,
Wellingborough, Northamptonshire, NN8 2RQ, England.*

Printed in Great Britain by Richard Clay Limited, Bungay, Suffolk

3   5   7   9   10   8   6   4   2

CONTENTS

The aim of this little book is to show you proven ways to help yourself feel better than you do ...

1.

THINKING POSITIVE
Affirmations and Visualizations

NEGATIVITY IS SELF-DESTRUCTIVE
The title of this section was the first sign I saw on my first visit to the Indian ashram that was later to become my home. It was inscribed in large letters and I understood it intellectually. But it was not till some years later that I 'got' it — 'getting it' being experiencing directly the truth of an otherwise abstract proposition 'in my bones', a connecting-up of ten sounds of syllables with the way it is and the way I am. It was more than insight, more like certainty.

This valuable learning experience was occasioned by a fierce quarrel with a friend which ended with my storming off on my bicycle (*everyone* rides bicycles in India) in the direction of the river. I was heading for the burning-ghats where I had been often before to meditate, a quiet place and usually deserted but for the crows. It was night-time and just light enough to see as I pedalled angrily along the lonely path, re-running the video of the quarrel in my head with a sound-track more in my favour than had actually been the case. Suddenly, two shapes erupted snarling from an isolated cottage I was passing and pursued me, hair on end, snapping at my legs. But then my hair was too, for they were large, emaciated and possibly rabid dogs who obviously meant business. Fortunately, they kept pace with me on the same side. Unable to shake them off I managed to dismount without getting my right leg bitten and for the next ten minutes literally kept them at bay with the bicycle, snarling and shouting back at them as loud as I could, out of breath yet knowing instinctively that this was the only way to get out of this scary and dangerous situation. Lunging at them repeatedly with the bicycle, I was dimly aware of a feeling of centering, of strength arising within me. As I shouted louder, willing them to leave me alone, abruptly they turned and loped away into the darkness, to my surprise and intense relief.

Animals are sensitive to vibrations put out by humans, as any cat-lover will know. So are other human beings and indeed the whole environment. Since that experience I have observed over the years a definite correlation between the situations I find myself in and the nature of the energy I am putting out. Positive attitudes attract positive energy, negative attitudes attract negative energy. It is as if our environment is tuned exactly to our wavelength and beams back at us, magnified, the message we are transmitting. This realization is in fact a part of our collective experience: it is the essential message of Buddha and intrinsic to the law of karma; it is illustrated for us by Jesus in sayings such as, 'As ye reap, so shall ye sow' and, 'Those who live by the sword shall die by the sword'. It has passed into proverbs, those often under-rated storehouses of human experience, such as, 'Everybody loves a lover' and, 'Laugh and the whole world laughs with you. Cry, and you cry alone'.

But, as with the dogs as opposed to the ashram sign, you have to see it for yourself to be able to live by it. It is not at all a question of morality, of meeting other people's expectations, of being 'good'. It is about not giving yourself a bad time if you can possibly avoid it.

Experiment 1
Over the next few days, whenever anything particularly pleasant or unpleasant happens to you, try to remember to reflect as to whether you can trace any connection between it and what you were thinking, feeling, saying or doing before it happened. A good time to do this is before you go to sleep, reviewing the events of the day. No guilt, no blame; just report any connection as if it concerned a friend. With practice and increased awareness you will get to see these connections soon after the situation has arisen and eventually you will be able to anticipate them.

Experiment 2
As soon as you awake in the morning make a resolution that, come what may, you will enjoy yourself throughout the day. Repeat your resolution firmly to yourself with the idea that your word is law and that nobody can stop you doing what you really want to do. At intervals during the morning, whenever you

remember, repeat your resolution with the same confidence. Then observe what happens for the rest of the day. You, and the people with whom you communicate, are in for a pleasant surprise.

Experiment 3
This time on awakening give a good belly-laugh and keep on laughing for ten minutes. At first you will feel that the laugh is false, mirthless. Laugh on through this resistance and eventually you will start laughing in earnest. After all, a grown-up lying in bed splitting his or her sides with glee is not exactly serious. Remember this feeling of non-seriousness and recall how it felt during the course of the day. Acting how you would like to feel actually makes you feel that way.

NEGATIVE ATTITUDES NURTURE DIS-EASE
Anger and fear are not in themselves self-destructive. Indeed, their function is to protect our life, freedom, individuality or space by mobilizing the energy necessary for fight or flight. The stimulus of a situation interpreted as extremely threatening triggers off a marvellously complex physiological process involving the whole body which has received the signal: 'All Systems Go!' We tense our muscles to which the heart is pumping blood as fast as it can, contract our bellies to protect vital organs, dilate our pupils so as to locate better the source of the threat or the best avenue of escape, break out into a cold sweat and so on. In moments of total anger or fear we become whole and alive, charged with energy.

The choices before us are fourfold: to confront, retire, surrender or acknowledge that what was perceived as a threat was not so in reality. Unfortunately we are rarely total, either in experiencing what we're experiencing or in action. We are not conditioned to trust our own feelings and to express them directly. Women are perhaps more inhibited by upbringing to showing anger, men perhaps fear; we are all afraid to surrender to *anything* and hate to be proved wrong or look a fool. Thus the pure energy of a primary emotion is unresolved in pure action and thus unresolved hovers around in a limbo of nagging resentment or chronic anxiety.

In the descriptive phrase of Fritz Perls, founder of gestalt therapy, we don't 'shit or get off the pot'. Thus constipated, we poison our system with the toxins of negativity, destroying our own peace of mind by brooding and that of those around us by blaming. Instead of using our energy creatively we leak it. Drained, unable to relax and enjoy, we exhaust our batteries. Illness is not far away.

SYMPTOMS ARE BODY LANGUAGE

In the next chapter you will be introduced to structures and processes which will equip you with techniques for discharging negative energy harmlessly and for bringing clarity to the sources of it. We must first look at how illness can manifest in the body as a result of stress and its underlying mental attitudes.

Chronic Tension: arteriosclerosis, high blood pressure, thrombosis, coronaries, migraine, ulcers.

Resentment: jaundice, hepatitis, liver problems, cancer, tumours, arthritis, bone problems, rheumatism, shoulder pain, fevers, boils, abscesses, sinus trouble, headaches, mouth ulcers, teeth problems, throat infections.

Anxiety: asthma, chest problems, skin trouble, bladder problems, digestive disorders, shingles, cataracts, eye problems, fainting, throat problems.

Grief: acute depression, cancer, heart ailments, throat problems.

Guilt: acute depression, alcoholism, stroke, VD, prostate trouble, menstrual or menopause problems, warts, skin problems.

Virtually any mental attitude which results in blocking the free flow of body energy may lead to self-intoxication. Here are more examples:

Perfectionism, Narrow-mindedness, Hypercriticism, Meanness: brain tumour, ear problems, arteriosclerosis, headaches, constipation, problems of fingers and nails.
Feeling trapped: asthma, chest problems, acute depression.
Inflexibility: neck problems, knee problems.
Feeling overburdened, unsupported: shoulder pain, slipped disc, back pain, leg troubles, varicose veins, low blood pressure, colds, 'flu, virtually anything, including accidents!
Indecision: anaemia, teeth problems, foot problems.

The above is a short list intended not to alarm but to enlighten. They may not happen to you in that particular way or indeed at all, but they *could*. If you already are suffering from illness whether or not included in the list take comfort from the knowledge that what you are doing to yourself you may be able to undo.

DECODING THE MESSAGE OF SYMPTOMS

A word of warning is in place here. Throughout this section of the book I am assuming that if you are concerned about your health you will have already consulted a qualified practitioner of allopathic or homoeopathic medicine, or perhaps a registered acupuncturist. Only when you have learnt again the art of dialogue with your body and recovered sufficient sensitivity to its messages and confidence in your affirmations, to be described later, will you no longer require their services. In the meantime, the insight and positive energy gained from body awareness, affirmations and visualizations will make you feel better and speed recovery, whatever the form of treatment prescribed.

AWARENESS EXERCISE: DECODING SYMPTOMS

Slowly read through the list of mental attitudes and the ways in which they may manifest as illness. Pause after each condition, refer back to the attitude it relates to and notice if you feel there is a connection. Don't try too hard; rather relax and play with it, moving on if nothing comes or you experience resistance in any form.

Body language preceded speech and writing and the attempts of the latter to communicate states of mind and feeling often have recourse to allusions to the physical sensations which may accompany them. Here are some; see if you can find more.

broken-hearted
choked with anger/grief
eaten away by envy/resentment
boiling with anger
a lump in the throat
picking fault
stiff-necked, a pain in the neck
anaemic, wishy-washy
tight-assed
chew it over
he/she won't see reason

If we consider the functions of various parts of the body, the statements they may be making about our life-style and habits by malfunctioning can come through loud and clear. The psychic equivalents of the purely physical functions can give us a clue as to the area of our lives in which we are 'stuck' and to which we need to bring some clarity and change.

Head — thinking, judgements, values, ideas
Face — individuality, expressiveness, visibility
Eyes — seeing, looking
Nose — filtering out irritating substances
Ears — hearing, listening, letting in the outside world
Mouth — nourishment, taking in, talking
Teeth — biting on, breaking down for assimilation
Neck — flexibility, seeing all sides
Throat — self-expression
Shoulders — carrying burdens, punching
Chest — taking in and giving out, breathing-space, the seat of feeling and emotion, freedom and oppression
Arms — reaching out, self-defence
Hands — giving and taking, manipulating, grasping
Fingers — pointing, picking
Internal organs — assimilation and rejection, discrimination between what is nourishing and what isn't, the seat of anger, bile, gall, 'guts'
Bladder, anus — holding on, letting go
Genitals — pleasure, social identity and rôle
Back — carrying burdens, support, 'backbone'
Legs — support, movement, 'holding your ground'
Bones — structure, support, flexibility, movement
Feet — grounding, 'stepping out', kicking

LISTEN TO YOUR BODY

The functions of the parts of the body listed above are purposely left general. For the suggestions to be of any real use for you in creating a healthy and satisfying life-style you are the only person 'on the inside' to realize their significance for the unique being that you are. For example, if your intuition tells you that you are stagnating (or constipated) because you are holding on to something that you are unwilling to let go of, change will not start to happen until you dare to look at who or what it is that you are clinging to. It may be a relationship that you know deep down is a disaster but at least stops you being alone, an ideal that you have a lot invested in but in which you no longer believe, or grief at the loss of a loved one.

If you have contacted the feeling of oppression behind your persistent or recurring chest infection then look into who or what is oppressing you. Go deeper and deeper into the sensation of being shut in, trapped or whatever the taste of the feeling is for you and see exactly how you oppress yourself by saying yes when you mean no, over-committing yourself, accepting other people's authority and time-limits and not allowing yourself space to breathe.

You may find that the psychic equivalent of your illness or symptom is quite unrelated to what actually manifests in your body in terms of our lists. The important thing is that you are getting in touch with what you need in your life. At this moment you may need attention, reassurance, love and by falling ill you may be getting it. Next time, now you know, you may simply ask for it.

AFFIRMATIONS

Illness is a breakdown of communication. What you have been asked to do so far is to show your body that you are willing to re-open communication; you find usually that it will meet you more than half-way. You have to learn to listen to it first before it is willing to trust you again, to treat it with love and respect instead of poisoning it with negativity and neglect.

An affirmation is a positive statement about ourselves or about the world about us which, to the extent that we believe it and charge it with energy, can transform our experience in a profound and seemingly miraculous way. Not only will we feel better immediately, subjectively: our bodies respond to positive and accurate reprogramming by abandoning now out-dated symptoms and healing themselves; relationships and situations hitherto a problem will resolve themselves when seen from a new perspective; most magical of all, the environment starts coming up with things we hoped would happen plus some that open up new and hitherto unsuspected opportunities for us.

Affirmations work by replacing a negative programme in the computer that is mind by a positive, life-affirming one. Once you have started bringing awareness to your life and uncovering your self-limiting if not self-destructive tapes, you are ready to use affirmations to cancel them out. They can bring nothing but blessings to you whatever your state of health; indeed, their possibilities in bringing even spontaneous remission of terminal cancer have attracted the attention of the media.

EXAMPLES OF AFFIRMATIONS

I deserve to enjoy radiant health.

Every moment that passes I am feeling stronger and more alive.

The world is a loving place and I am at home here.

I am grateful for being alive and enjoy myself more every day.

I forgive with all my heart everyone who has ever hurt me and wish them well.

I am totally lovable just for being who I am.

I express my love and creativity in my work.

The world is an abundant place and I deserve to be prosperous.

I love and accept myself totally, just as I am right now.

I am completely free to create my life as I choose.

I let go of the old and welcome the new.

Life is fun. I live my life sincerely but without seriousness.

I see with loving eyes everyone and everything about me.

I can relax into life and trust that it loves me.

I drop the past and trust the future will bring me all I need.

I am overflowing with peace, joy and love.

I enjoy my sexuality and my manliness/womanliness.

There is no need to rush. I have always been here and I shall always be here.

I respect myself just for being who I am.

There is no need for guilt. Everything happens as it should.

It is OK to take time and space to do what I want to do.

Nobody has power over me. I am totally free.

I can express myself freely and with confidence.

I have the courage to stand up for myself.

It really is OK for me to have a good time.

Make an affirmation whenever you catch yourself starting to work up negative energy, for example, getting impatient while waiting for a bus, blaming yourself for something and putting yourself down in your head. Make affirmations when you have an insight into a mechanical habit that works against you in getting what you want. Make affirmations when you are 'down' or sick, having first listened to your body for clues as to why you *are* sick.

The more aware you become of your own process the more 'on target' your affirmations will be. The signs of how close you are to what your body needs to hear will be the degree of warm relaxation and relief or the sense of lightness and something lifting that you experience throughout your body. With certain direct-hit affirmations there is sometimes a rush of energy which might express itself in laughter or a desire to dance. Enjoy yourself.

RESISTANCE TO AFFIRMATIONS

Choose affirmations which are positive about yourself and loving to others or they will rebound on yourself. They are not wishful thinking but more like a depth-charge of positive energy that will disperse the negative conditioning below the surface that has hitherto manipulated your way of seeing and behaviour. The amount of resistance you encounter will be in direct proportion to the strength of that conditioning and the extent that you are identified with and unwilling to let go of the tape to be erased.

Resistance may take the form of difficulty in concentrating on the affirmation or in saying it, a draining-away of energy or a feeling of hopelessness or disbelief that it will work for you. If you really do want to get well or taste a new way of being, persist. After all, what have you got to lose?

It is not necessary to know how affirmations work for them to transform your life; it is necessary only to believe that they do work and to actualize them in ways that will shortly be suggested. For those who need some 'juice' to get them in the right frame of mind for making an affirmation with any credibility to themselves it may be helpful to browse through the following seed ideas.

FOR YOUR CONSIDERATION. . .

Jesus said:

> Faith can move mountains.
> Thy *faith* has made thee whole.
> By your words you will be justified and by your words you shall be condemned.
> To them that hath it shall be given. From them that hath not it shall be taken away.

You get what you put out — multiplied.
We create our own world by what we think is true.
For us, our own word is law.
Energy follows intention.

Attention is energy. Whatever you choose to give your attention to becomes more real for you.

ACTUALIZING AFFIRMATIONS

Make your affirmation slowly and firmly as many times as necessary to cut through your own resistance. Stop when it feels right and rest, confident that you have cleared the rubbish-heap in your garden and planted a seed. In the days that follow nourish the seed by repeating the affirmation a few times with conviction and directing positive energy to it. Resist the temptation to get obsessed with it; trust that it is taking root. Rather, start acting as if what you were affirming is already the case; get the feeling in your body that you are already how you wanted to be.

When familiar situations arise and you start to react in the old way, remind yourself of your decision to be in the world in a new way and act on it. It is scary because it is unfamiliar; you will feel vulnerable and, surprisingly, maybe a little sad, for the old you is dying.

As your new way of being becomes integrated you will forget you ever made the affirmation. You have arrived.

VISUALIZATIONS

Visualizations can be used alone or in conjunction with affirmations. Like the latter, they are being used at the Bristol and the other Cancer Help Centres. The patient is asked to visualize the tumour in any way that feels right, to sense its size, shape, texture, colour, exact location and so on, and then to create in the mind's eye that growth under attack by the drug with which the sufferer is being treated. Guided by the therapist they produce their own home movie with a happy ending, the complete disappearance of the cancer. The process may take many sessions, in the course of which the patient experiences his or her own resistance to getting well and is helped to overcome it and flood the body with the positive energy it desperately needs.

Experiment 4: The disappearing headache
This experiment will be familiar to those who have taken the est training.

If you have a headache that you wish to get rid of, find a comfortable position and relax as much as the pain will allow.

Have the conscious intention to make the headache disappear. Now try to feel the intensity of the pain as much as you can. Is it sharp, dull, continuous or intermittent? Find its exact location, size, shape and boundaries: how many inches inside your head is it? What colour is it — try to *see* it. As you watch the pain it will keep changing size, and possibly location. Stay with it, watching it expand, contract, change colour and texture, maybe suddenly erupting into a shower of sparks or streamers as if in an effort to shake you off. If you persist it will eventually shrink and become less vivid. Soon it will be down to a dot. By then you will suddenly realize your headache has gone. The reason? Whatever you experience totally, disappears.

Visualizations are even more powerful than affirmations, for they speak the same dream language as the mind. As with affirmations be careful only to feed attention, i.e. energy, to positive images. Similarly, their effectiveness in bringing about changes you want in your life, be it health, the experience of prosperity, love or whatever, depends on the clarity and feeling quality you bring to the visualizations and the certainty in your bones that they will most certainly materialize on the physical plane. Never visualize harming anybody else, for your own good.

To make a visualization is to consciously and lovingly use the creative law by which focused energy gives form to ideas. In the Bible it is expressed as 'The Word was made flesh'. I am actualizing the law at this moment, creating a book from invisible ideas in my head by feeding them attention and intention to communicate them on paper. I am surrounded in my room by objects that began their journey into material existence as similarly invisible ideas in a craftsman's head; as he worked with attention and intention the energy became denser until — well, there's my wastepaper basket. And so with houses and cities themselves — all a manifestation of mind.

THE LAW OF EFFECT

To actualize your visualization, start acting as if it had already materialized. This is to make use of the law of effect. This quite illogical yet none the less real law states: 'Produce the effect and the cause will follow'. Try it for yourself by practising experiments 2 and 3 if you have not already done so. Three things are needed to attract anything you need into your life: intention (being clear and specific as to exactly what you need and by when); trust (believing totally that it will surely manifest); expectation (feeling and acting as if it was already happening). A visualization is a deliberate creation with focused energy behing it; acting it out with awareness will attract the experiences and mobilize resources you need to make it a reality.

An example. If you are experiencing poverty in your life, take time to examine carefully your basic beliefs about money, especially negative ones. Do you believe that it is hard to come by? That there is a limited supply in the world and that your gain is another's loss? That to want money is sordid, unspiritual or 'uncool'? How do you relate to money on a feeling level? Are you anxious, more concerned with saving for a rainy day than enjoying what it can give you? Are you mean, or unable to stop it running through your fingers? Are you embarrassed at negotiating a price for something you are selling or a fee for your services? Is it OK for you to be rich or at least well-off?

When you find your basic block to prospering yourself, compose an appropriate affirmation which will counteract the negative tape. Make your affirmation in the usual way and actualize it in everyday life. You may well find that your negative tape is more to do with you than with money itself, for example, 'I don't deserve to be comfortably off' or even 'I wouldn't have anything to complain about if I had a lot of money!'

Visualize your present financial situation and what has led up to it. How would you like it to be different right now? Visualize in as much detail as possible how you would like to be dressed, where you would like to be living, the things you would surround yourself with if you had money to your heart's content. Enjoy yourself. Most important of all, allow the *feel* of prosperity, of abundance and freedom from worry to permeate your body. Persist with the visualization, cutting through any resistance. You will know when to stop, feeling more like the emperor you are than the beggar you were.

Actualizing this particular visualization would include, first of all, being grateful for all the things you already have which you take for granted. You may realize that wealth is relative and that you were in fact richer than you thought. Break old patterns of meanness and anxiety without going overboard. Take a taxi if it's raining or you are in a hurry — and tip well. In shops, buy the best rather than the cheapest food or clothes.

Give yourself small treats, and treat others. Remember, what you give you get back, multiplied: 'good measure, pressed down, shaken together and running over' will be poured into your lap. Money attracts money and, as every businessman or punter knows, you have to lay it out to get it back. And get it back you will, whether in a better job, having passed the interview on the strength of your smart appearance and your confidence in your own ability and positive attitude, or from some new, unexpected source. Money is energy; it likes to move. Move it with awareness.

2.

RELIEVING NEGATIVE FEELINGS
Techniques for Harmless Emotional Catharsis

EXPRESS YOUR FEELINGS WITH AWARENESS

We have seen how negative mental attitudes are toxic for the body and how to combat them with positive affirmations and visualizations. Sometimes, however, we may be so flooded with strong negative feelings that it is impossible to connect in any real way with positivity at that moment. The body needs to cathart first, that is, to discharge the emotion by expressing the energy generated by it in action or movement and sound. In this section we examine techniques used in co-counselling, encounter groups, primal and gestalt therapy for working through your anger, jealousy, and so on, effectively, neither 'dumping' them on others nor crippling yourself by repression.

CO-COUNSELLING

This technique combines the relief from discharging emotion and gaining insight with the therapeutic benefits of trusting self-disclosure to a sympathetic listener, something we tend to do anyway when upset. To choose to be transparent, with awareness, has its own therapeutic value. The 'sharing' that figures so largely in therapy groups and other systems like est or 'enlightenment intensives' is reminiscent of the confessional. The important difference, however, is that the seeker comes from a place not of conformity and guilt, feeling 'wrong', but of self-direction and self-expression and resulting self-discovery.

Since, strictly speaking, the techniques in this book are limited to those one can learn and practise alone, co-counselling is described in the appendix. It is unique though, in that both partners are 'amateurs' and are there for each other on a non-professional, non-fee-paying basis. The one-to-one communication of co-counselling differs too from orthodox psychotherapy in that each partner is on an equal footing. There is no transference of responsibility, no interpretations according to concepts of normality/abnormality or differing schools of psychoanalysis.

EXPRESS FEELINGS DIRECTLY

Whenever possible, express your feelings directly at the time they arise. If this is hard for you it may help to know that it is for most people. We are conditioned by our upbringing to be phoney, to fear loss of love if we are authentic rather than to be honest, to manipulate and blame others rather than to be authentically expressive and take responsibility for who we are. As a result we repress our emotions. Therapy groups are about risking the latter in a safe and supportive environment, by sharing your expectations and needs directly and being 'up front' with your real feelings about other participants and their games. It works both ways: they too will share their expectations of you and 'feedback' on how you come across to them. To participate in a good therapy group can be an enlightening experience.

However, 'real life' is not a therapy group. Structures used in these groups are useful in again flexing the muscles of authentic self-expression. But to exercise them on the boss at work or indiscriminately on others can lead to unpleasant results: you might lose your job or frighten away people not prepared to play encounter games with you. However, some of the structures used in encounter and gestalt groups can be used with beneficial results working on your own. The important factor in the transformation of negative energy into positive energy is catharsis, i.e. the discharging of that energy harmlessly. Emotional equilibrium follows and with it insight and revaluation.

HOW TO DISCHARGE ANGER
WITHOUT HURTING ANYONE

Let us assume you are furious and unwilling or unable to express this directly at the time, for whatever reason. It may be that you have received bad news or that it is inappropriate to vent your ill humour on the boss, a child or an ailing aged mother who has incurred your wrath.

Remembering 'least said, soonest mended', withdraw to a room where you can be alone and, preferably, where you can make as much noise as you like without disturbing others. Give yourself permission to feel your anger totally. Lie on a mattress on your back and throw a childish tantrum, kicking and beating the mattress with your fists. Start slowly, beating alternately with right arm/left arm, then left or right leg. Let go and continue way past the time you are breathless and want to stop. If the anger doesn't come or you feel inhibited it helps to keep saying, 'I'm angry, I'm angry'.

If you prefer, kneel on the floor with a large cushion in front of you. Raise your arms, make fists and start beating hell out of the cushion. You may prefer to use a tennis racket. Put your whole body into the action and let a sound come as you hit. It doesn't have to be words — a snarl will do nicely! Keep on until you are totally exhausted.

A third method is to strangle a small cushion to death or 'wring the neck' of a towel; once again, it is important to use your total strength. Don't stop breathing as this cuts off the flow of feeling. If you can, roar or shout whatever comes. If you have to be quiet you can discharge verbal aggression by biting hard on a sheet or pillow while squeezing or wringing it with your hands. Don't sleep on that pillow again, however, until it has been aired and the pillow-slip laundered: it will be charged with toxic energy and you are likely to have bad dreams or awake with a headache!

Allow yourself as much time as you need to get clear of your anger. You will feel when to stop. Lie down on your back, take a few deep breaths and relax. Let your mind wander back to the situation that provoked such a strong reaction from you. Visualize your antagonist, remember the words that passed between you and the feelings you felt. Allow yourself to feel them again. As you taste them more and more fully, ask yourself what it was *really* about. How *exactly* were you threatened by what happened? What was behind your anger? Is the truth really that you felt hurt, let down, unloved? What were your expectations that on this occasion were not met? Ask yourself whether they were reasonable expectations. Even if they were, you have learnt a valuable lesson, namely, that life does not always meet your expectations, reasonable or unreasonable.

Next time you meet the person who 'made' you angry you have a choice whether or not to broach the subject. If you do, remember there is a big difference between saying something about yourself and stating something about another. The former is a sharing, the latter an attack which usually provokes a defensiveness and counter-attack. This is ping-pong, not communication. Remember too that your feelings are *your* feelings: nobody has the power to *make* you feel anything, including anger.

We all carry unresolved anger around with us from past hurts and put-downs, just waiting for a chance to dump it on somebody. We can go through our lives like a baleful jukebox blaring out the same discordant tune whenever somebody 'pushes our button'. With awareness we can change the record: but first catharsis may be necessary.

HANDLING JEALOUSY

The hurt that is often hidden behind explosive anger is usually more readily uncovered when working with jealousy, that most painful and destructive of emotions. Our pain lies in being torn between love and hate and experiencing being thus split is the essential ingredient of most of the mental suffering of the human race. The particular destructiveness of jealousy stems from the fact that we are usually loath to admit it. As a result the energy it generates comes out 'sideways' in nagging and possessiveness which serve to alienate further the very person to whom we are looking for love.

As with anger, start by throwing a tantrum or beating a cushion. If you allow your breathing to bring out your real feelings, however, you are likely to get in touch with your hurt. Flow with the new feeling and let your relationship with the cushion change accordingly. Imagine your partner, lover or whomsoever you are jealous of, as the cushion. Give yourself permission to hug, kiss or strangle him or her. Have a dialogue with him/her as the cushion. Speak from the heart: you don't have to be hostile here or play cool to hide your own vulnerability. Do it for *you*.

Having shared your real feelings, needs and expectations, change over. Be your partner talking to you (you may like to provide another cushion to represent yourself as you sit on the first cushion). How would he/she respond to what you have just shared? How does he/she see you? Keep changing sides, sharing with each other and see what comes up. By the time you feel 'finished', the way you see the relationship may have radically changed. You may have decided there is nothing in it for you and take the responsibility for ending it. Or your 'partner' may have convinced you that you really are loved and need to be more trusting. Whatever comes up, you will certainly feel less of a victim and more in touch with your needs. Next time you feel jealous, remember what you have learned in this process and *choose* whether to make a scene or ask for what you need.

TECHNIQUES FOR 'DEFUSING' OTHER NEGATIVE STATES

The basic technique is to give yourself permission in a safe environment to experience the feeling *totally,* with appropriate expressive action, using your whole body. Don't hold your breath or you will numb yourself to feeling; rather, breathe through the mouth, allowing sighs and sounds to come. Whatever is experienced totally, disappears, as we discovered in experiment 4. This applies as much to unpleasant emotional states as to headaches, but first you have to ride the horse in the direction it is going. Initially it is easier to do this by externalizing what you are experiencing and in some cases verbalizing the dialogue going on in your head.

By applying these techniques whenever you feel 'out of your depth' and controlled by inner emotional turmoil you will quickly find relief and equilibrium, as well as learning to trust letting go into the flow of your own energy-process. Eventually you will identify less with your feelings and not feel so compelled to act them out: with this non-identification comes insight and choice. You are on the way to becoming a self-observer, another name for a meditator. How to go further into meditation will be described in a later section. Meanwhile, here are more examples of gestalt techniques.

GUILT/DEPRESSION: Both of these are the subjective experience of a turning in of anger. Their common features are self-rejection, self-torture and contraction. We often get relief from our own tensions by laying them out on others; we treat them the way we treat ourselves. If I feel bad I am not likely to enjoy the spectacle of you feeling good and will probably try to bring you down. Apply this principle harmlessly to your cushion by doing to it what you are doing to yourself. Depress it, i.e. make a depression in it by hitting it or boring into it with clenched fists, putting all your strength behind them. Breathe.

Go on boring or punching, letting out sounds to express your frustration, disgust or despair.

Put the person who is 'making' you feel guilty on the cushion and have a dialogue in which you share your feelings and resentment at his/her expectations. Change places and reply to your own recriminations from the other's point of view. Keep swapping over until the energy has gone out of it. You may start to feel bored with the whole business or achieve insight into who is *really* doing what to whom.

GRIEF: Unresolved grief can be quite lethal. If one does not literally die of a 'broken heart' or its equivalent, a coronary, excessive mourning with its attendant depression, loss of appetite and the will to live can seriously deplete the life-force and lay one wide open to debilitating illness. Tied up with the sense of loss is a whole complex of other feelings: guilt at not having been always loving towards the departed one, whether deceased or deserting; anger and fear at being left alone; jealousy, loss of self-esteem if a lover or spouse has moved into a new relationship. The therapeutic technique here is firstly to express everything that still needs to be shared with the lost loved one, verbally and non-verbally, and then to say goodbye, in whichever way feels right.

ANXIETY/WORRY: Persistent worrying is not only exhausting, it can make you ill, as we have seen in Chapter One. It is a chronic leaking of energy and depletes our reserves as pure physical exertion never does. In fact strenuous exercise, if enjoyed, actually relaxes and charges the body, as sportsmen will know.

Anxiety arises from lack of trust that we are capable of responding appropriately to situations spontaneously. Unwilling to relax and deal with each situation as it presents itself, we 'rehearse' in advance, trying to forestall being caught with our pants down. Fritz Perls, in another descriptive phrase, called anxiety 'stage-fright': a typical anxiety dream is of being an actor 'drying up' on stage before an audience. Others are of sitting an examination unprepared or of being held up in traffic, late for an extremely important appointment.

Once again the technique is to do deliberately and totally what we are doing half-heartedly and with resistance. Rehearse with awareness and enjoy playing out your catastrophic expectations with non-seriousness. Conjure up your worst fears, exaggerate and parody them. If your anxiety is diffuse rather than specific, play your nervous and perplexed sub-personality to the hilt, gibbering and shaking with fear. Use your whole body.

Move around the room, darting in simulated panic from corner to corner; cringe wide-eyed in corners, making yourself as small as possible. Stand in front of a mirror and study your body and facial expression as you ham it up. Unless you are quite humourless you will soon start to laugh at your own reflection. We are all in the same boat: to be human is to be vulnerable and it is not given to us to foresee the future. Don't blame yourself for it.

When you start feeling more confident, give your body a good shake to rid it of the nervous energy you have generated. Shake arms and legs vigorously and perform the meridian massage and aura cleaning processes described in a later chapter. These should be done after each of the cathartic techniques described in this section. Also, after catharting it is good to shower and change your clothes.

If worry persists, have a dialogue with 'worry' on cushions. Perhaps it has a message for you that you need to hear. It could be that you need to make some life-style changes, for example to slow down or be less extravagant. Listen to it with sincerity and openness and then decide either to take its advice or to drop it. Next time you find it starting to take you over, remind it of your decision.

OVER BURDENED/UNDER PRESSURE: Anything under pressure contracts or implodes. The technique here is therefore to go with it by tightening all muscles and contracting the whole body, making yourself as small as possible. In this structure holding the breath is appropriate: you really don't have breathing space in your life. Huddle yourself into a ball on the bed or the floor and tighten and squeeze as hard as you can. Hug yourself. There will come a point where you feel you can contract no further. If you persist, eventually you will *ex*plode. Enjoy the sudden expansion, jump, dance, stretch, laugh, sing. Express with your total being what release is for you. Feel the space around you. Stretch out your arms, stand on tiptoe; take up as much of that space for yourself as you can. Breathe fully and deeply and let out sighs.

When you are ready, lie down, close your eyes and relax. Reflect for a while on the pressures in your life and visualize yourself in those situations. Ask yourself how you managed to create situations in which you are overburdened and what you could do to allow yourself more space and time.

Take a pen and paper and make a list of your priorities and ways to apportion your time and energy in ways more satisfying to you. Be especially aware of what is behind your workaholic self-driving and your eagerness to take on new commitments. What is in it for you? What are you trying to prove? What needs are you trying to fill by driving yourself to exhaustion: recognition? love? security? Make up affirmations to give these things to yourself.

Examine your conditioning about work: has it extolled the virtues of drudgery rather than creativity? Is it acceptable to you to choose your own work and to enjoy it? Do you feel guilty when you take things easy or relax? Affirmations here are the key to transforming your experience from being burdened to enjoying responsibility and putting out creative energy from a place of initiator rather than victim.

INDECISION: This can be an agonizing state and, for Librans like myself, a familiar one. To end a relationship that is going through a bad patch or to put more living energy into it? To go back to India during the hot season and monsoon or to stay and enjoy Spring and Summer in Europe? Indecision is about not wanting to make 'mistakes' and being unable to see the future except in terms of the past. We might miss out. For example, the week I spend writing this chapter *could* have been enjoyably spent in Ibiza. Memories of the past come back of swimming in the bluest of seas at Salinas beach and relaxing over evening aperitifs at Mariano's. What it would in fact have been like I have no way of knowing. Possibly rainy, crowded and unpleasant. Certainly not exactly the same as I have known it in the past.

The first thing to direct attention to when crippled with indecision is the source of the pressure. Why the hurry? You may have to tolerate uncertainty as to your future in order to give yourself time to come up with a direction. Perhaps you just don't have enough information yet on which to act; perhaps the time is not yet ripe for action and the wisest course is to do nothing.

If you really *do* have to act fast, consider each possibility in turn, visualizing it in as much detail as possible. Be aware of the response that comes up in your body and feelings, however slight. There should be a perceptible shift in feeling response to each projected course of action and this will give you clues as to what you *really* want to do. A pull towards pleasurable anticipation or a relaxing is a sign to go ahead; a tightening up, a 'down' feeling in your body, is a hint that this one is not for you. The more you trust this feeling level of response the clearer will become the messages, for you are going beyond mind and exercising the muscles of intuition — the part of you which 'knows'. You can tap this reservoir of innate wisdom further by doing the following visualization exercise:

The Wise Old Man

Relax, close your eyes: take a few deep breaths. Consider the question to which you need an answer and frame it in words to yourself.

Visualize yourself out in the country. It is a beautiful day. The sun is shining from a clear sky; it is warm and yet a gentle breeze refreshes you as you walk through a meadow which is bright with buttercups and green, green grass. Birds sing as you cross the meadow and start to climb a rather steep hill. Winding your way up the path, occasionally pausing to rest, you tell yourself that you have come to consult the oracle who lives on this hill. He is renowned all over the world as a man of uncanny insight and wisdom, which in his compassion he is willing to share with those who seek him out.

Continuing up the hill you eventually reach the top. You pause to survey the marvellous view before scanning the hill-top for the oracle's abode. Sure enough, you espy a sort of grotto, a small cave, which forms the very summit of the hill. You venture inside: it is cool, still and an atmosphere of peace reigns. On a rock, sitting in a most relaxed way and smiling in welcome is a man dressed in a simple white robe. His face is at the same time old and childlike, showing both his wisdom and innocence: you feel instinctively that he is both 'as wise as a serpent and innocent as a dove' and that you have known him all your life. In a gentle voice he asks: 'Anything to say to me?' Look into his eyes and ask your question. Then listen to his reply.

After visualizations as deep as this one, remember to take a few minutes afterwards to bring yourself back, otherwise you may feel disoriented if you rejoin others immediately or go out into the street. Feel your body, open your eyes, look slowly around the room taking in objects, take a few deep breaths. Consider the answer you have received.

If your oracle did not answer, that *was* your answer. Maybe you need to look at the question from a different angle. Perhaps the truth is that you don't really *want* an answer. If you feel this is true, ask yourself how the present stalemate about which you complain is in fact serving your secret needs. What are you getting out of not making any move right now? Take responsibility for not wanting to make a decision and enjoy floating. If you really are stuck, tolerate waiting until a clear direction comes. When it does it may come in a dream.

WORKING WITH YOUR DREAMS

After working through any of the above cathartic processes you are likely to dream that night. This is a sign that certain contents of your unconscious have been energized and need to be assimilated by the conscious mind or ego. A reshuffling is taking place in the psyche; new possibilities of being are becoming available to you and may be incorporated in your life-style if you allow them. Keep a notebook and pen by your bedside, ready for jotting down any dream you remember on awakening, in as much detail as possible.

Respect and value your dreams: they work for you to maintain psychic equilibrium, to guide you in the next stage of growth, sometimes to warn that you need to give more attention to neglected aspects of living. The weaver of dreams is that part of you that *knows,* represented in the last visualization exercise as the Wise Old Man. Readers familiar with Jung will recognize this archetype of the collective unconscious.

To the extent that we are not in touch with our own innate wisdom, we project it on 'wise old men' (or women) outside ourselves, whether psychotherapists, fortune-tellers or gurus. Unfortunately, unless they are enlightened, totally 'clear' what they have to tell us about ourselves, however intuitive or perceptive, is likely to be mixed with our own 'stuff' — projections, ego-trips, belief systems, moral judgements.

We can be guided on the way to self-realization, but ultimately only we ourselves can experience directly who we are. There is no real substitute for self-observation and dialogue with our own unconscious.

The holistic approach to dreams is experiential rather than analytical, as in psychiatry. The acupuncturist, for example, will be interested in the *texture* of the dream: does it show an emphasis on metal, for example, as opposed to earth, fire, water or wood? Are there metallic objects in the dream like guns, nails, motor-cars? Whereas a Freudian analyst would probably wallow in phallic symbolism, the acupuncturist would take these objects as clues to the correct treatment of the patient. He might infer that the emotional content of the dream was about the patient's unconscious grief at the *hardness* of life and that attention should be given to the organs associated in acupuncture with the element metal, namely lungs and colon.

Whatever the approaches, however, the most widely used technique of working with dreams is that of gestalt. The general approach of this alternative therapy, developed by Fritz Perls before his death in 1970, is outlined below.

THE GESTALT APPROACH TO DREAMS

The gestalt approach to dreams posits the following:
1. that everything you dream about is *you*, even other people, animals, objects and places;
2. that to the degree that these aspects of yourself are recognized and integrated you will experience more fullness of living;
3. that a dream is a parable about *you* couched in the preverbal language of imagery and association;
4. that the therapeutic value of working with a dream lies not in intellectual understanding of its symbolism but in re-experiencing consciously the feeling content of those symbols and images.

Leave the insight into the 'meaning' of the dream to come in its own time. Concentrate on feeling its message for you by identifying in turn with each constituent of the dream, by *becoming* it.

HOW TO 'GESTALT' YOUR DREAMS

Eyes closed, narrate your dream aloud in the first person and in the present tense, i.e. as if it were actually unfolding now. Here is an example, a recent dream of my own.

'I am wandering in an underground chamber in the earth, looking for something. It is a sort of catacomb hollowed out of the earth which forms its walls with two passages leading off to the left and right respectively. I first explore the passage to the left and join several young children who are playing there. They accept me without much curiosity but I am soon bored and retrace my steps to the central chamber. I notice a large flat-topped, very solid-looking table in the middle of the central chamber. There is nothing on it. I start to move into the right-hand tunnel in which there is an elderly couple. As I do so, suddenly a large dog, something like a Dalmatian, or a setter, materializes from the under-surface of the table and bounds towards me. He is not aggressive but tremendously exuberant and playful. He keeps leaping up at me to seize something I am holding away from him in my right hand. It is a large bar of chocolate, which I am reluctant to give to him.

'Eventually I realize that in his efforts to take the chocolate he has bitten my hand. It is bleeding slightly. Advancing into the right-hand passage I admonish the old man and woman for not restraining their dog. There is a sink with taps in the wall beside them. The dream ends with me washing the wound in my hand and reassuring the couple that it is nothing serious.'

The next step is to *become* each part of the dream in turn. Identify yourself and state what you are doing and why you are there, always in the present tense. If you get stuck, stay with it. Be open to the obvious, which may be unexpected simply because dream language can be very literal. My own work on this dream consisted in acting out the following roles and feeling their associations for me.

'I am a space inside the earth, hollowed out (by whom?). . . I am "earthy", of the earth "grounded". . . There are children in me and old people. . .'

'I am a child playing in the left-hand underground passage. I'm not very interested in other people. I just want to play. . .'

'I am a table. . . I'm heavy, solid, with nothing showing on the surface (what is a table *for*?) You can put things on me. Underneath me there's a powerful, very alive animal. . . Out of sight. . .'

'I am an old man/woman. I'm just "hanging out" in the right-hand passage. My dog is making himself a nuisance to others and I'm being held responsible. Should I keep him on a leash? But then, if that guy wasn't so mean in sharing his goodies (i.e. chocolate) he wouldn't have been bitten. . .'

'I am a dog, an animal. I came from under the table. I am an "under-dog". I'm strong, exuberant and playful. I enjoy my animal energy. I just want to have a good time and take whatever I feel like taking. I expect people to give me what I want. I bite the hand that doesn't feed me. . .'

By now associations should be coming thick and fast. Become the narrator again and have a dialogue in turn with each 'character'. You can use two cushions to represent yourself as the dreamer and yourself as the part of the dream. Talk to each other, and then allow each character to relate in turn to each of the others. Play with the dream in the days that follow, relive it, chew on its parts, extract the nourishment it offers your being and assimilate it into your consciousness.

For me this was an extraordinarily rich dream from which I quarried much of value for my personal life. Its message included reassessment of my goals and identifications. It pointed in the direction of 'going to earth', 'grounding', 'earthiness', rather than searching for 'spiritual' highs and peak experiences. The polarity between my 'child' and my 'parent' was straight out of a textbook on Transactional Analysis; following either was 'barking up (or in this case down) the wrong tree or tunnel'. The most alive part of me was my high-spirited animal, usually, however, kept tucked away under a rather austere surface (the table) which invited burdens to be laid on it by its lack of feature and its seeming strength and reliability. My unwillingness to play, to nourish the underside of this surface (i.e. the underdog) resulted in damage to my right hand, which I associated with relating to the world in a creative way. The end of the dream was a reminder to my parent not to be too serious.

Only you can 'interpret' your own dreams for they speak in your dialect, your idiom. They are probably the most intimate personal and true statement you are ever likely to make about yourself, albeit symbolically. Connecting with and owning this statement is a deeply satisfying and integrating experience, if often humbling. True insight transforms and gestalt is an awareness technique which provides us often with what its founder used to call 'Uh-hah' experiences — the 'uh-hah' being the gasp of astonishment and release on seeing something about how we are and what we do that was until now hidden from us by its very obviousness.

3.

THE ART OF SELF-NOURISHMENT
Diet and Relaxation

THE ART OF SELF-NOURISHMENT
Just as we can poison ourselves with our own negativity we can make ourselves ill by what we choose to assimilate from our environment. Wrong eating can kill us, other people's negativity can 'bring us down', uncongenial environments and intractable situations can make us seriously depressed or chronically tense. We have to learn to discriminate between the truly nourishing and the toxic, to be sensitive to our own biorhythms and needs, and to give ourselves permission to 'take our space' in the world.

THE WAY OF FOOD
The most obvious and basic form of self-nourishment is food. Yet very many people eat without awareness of the connection between their diet and the way they feel. Junk foods are prevalent in the affluent West: adulterated, devitalized and often saturated with sugar, their contribution to the modern epidemics of cancer, heart disease, arthritis and many others has only recently been alerted here.

Too often we eat unwisely and then seek relief in proprietary antacids, laxatives and 'settlers' as if the digestive system itself were to blame for our dis-ease. This is inevitable in a society where straight medicine is geared rather to suppressing symptoms than to holistic health and where a 'diet' is synonymous with more or less drastic purging following indiscriminate indulgence in toxic foods. Yet, for the yogi 'we are what we eat', while for pioneers of macrobiotics like Georges Ohsawa and Michio Kushi 'the Way of Food' is the basic approach to understanding and curing sickness of both body and mind.

In the USA food allergies have been researched and have been found to be the cause of much illness, including acute depression and schizophrenia. In this country, since Dr Richard Mackarness' study of food allergies published in 1976, there has been more interest shown in this field, the most significant breakthrough in the understanding and treatment of mental illness since the introduction of anti-depressant drugs in the 1950s. The first question to ask ourselves therefore if we are feeling 'down' or sick is: 'How and what have I been eating?'

WHAT TO EAT?

The main schools of thought today on eating for health are the following:

The Western 'Balanced' Diet

This, the most familiar diet to most people, is conceived in terms of ensuring an adequate supply of proteins, carbohydrates, fats, minerals and vitamins and in terms of calories for weight control. Excellent introductions to this approach are *Let's Eat Right to Keep Fit* and *Let's Get Well* (Unwin paperbacks) by Adelle Davis.

The Eastern Macrobiotic Approach

The macrobiotic 'way of food' is a system based on the concepts of yin and yang, the interplay of which polarities in Chinese philosophy account for all phenomena in the manifest world. Yin energy manifests as female, cool, dark, soft, yielding, passive; yang as male, hot, light, hard, aggressive, active. Yin corresponds to acid foods, yang to alkaline. Yin foods would include drinks, fruits, spicy, sweet or sour foods, summer-grown vegetables, green, blue or purple in colour. Yang are meat, fish and poultry, cereals, bitter or salty foods and autumn- or winter-grown vegetables which are hard and red, orange or yellow.

All foods have yin or yang properties and macrobiotics seek to balance their intake to avoid an extreme of either, for such imbalance is at the root of all dis-ease. Some foods should be completely avoided as toxic, for example the extremely yin vegetables tomatoes, aubergines, potatoes, which are related to deadly nightshade; milk, too, is considered a natural food only for babies.

An offshoot of Taoist philosophy, which emphasizes living in harmony with one's environment as a basic requirement for well-being and serenity, macrobiotics advise eating only food grown locally (or within 500 miles of one's home) and varying one's diet according to the season. Thus it frowns on eating, for example, tropical fruits and yet approves the intake of meat in winter or in cold climates. Its best-known injunction is to make grains — rice, whole wheat, rye, barley, oats, millet, maize, buckwheat — the staple diet, together with fresh vegetables, based on the ratio among human teeth of molars and incisors; and a view of agriculture as an activity peculiar to humans alone as a species. Macrobiotics is also a system of healing whose method is to restore the balance between yin and yang by controlled diet. The best introductions to macrobiotics are *Zen Macrobiotics* by Georges Ohsawa and *Natural Healing Through Macrobiotics* by Michio Kushi.

Vegetarianism

Vegetarians insist that eating meat is unacceptable on ethical and practical grounds. They claim that it entails suffering to animals on a gigantic scale and more so today because of the methods used in producing, for example, white veal, goose liver for pâté, and battery hens. The antibiotic used to forestall disease among closely-confined animals in large numbers is transferred to the human system together with the meat.

Finally, the amount of land needed for pasture is unproductive when compared with the yield of arable land in grains and vegetables. Vegans include in their ban on animal products dairy foods such as milk, cheese and eggs. They claim that protein deficiency in their diet can easily be avoided by including beans, pulses, and meat substitutes such as soy chunks, tofu, and nuts.

The Yogic Approach

The basis of this approach is summed up in the admonition: 'You are what you eat'. Like vegetarians, practitioners of yoga disapprove of meat but for slightly different reasons. They insist that the major cause of illness is self-intoxication through faulty elimination and hatha yoga includes in its discipline practices for the cleansing of the digestive tract from mouth to anus.

Meat is taboo on the grounds that it is hard to digest and assimilate and tends to putrefy in the bowel and produce toxins in the blood. More than that, the meat-eater absorbs the toxins released in the animal's blood by panic at the time of slaughter. Instead of taking in such negative vibrations along with dead flesh, the yogi prefers the positive and gentler vibrations of vegetables, nuts, fruits. Attention is also given to fasting as a means of purification, both of body and spirit.

Health Foods

The emphasis in health food stores is on natural foods (i.e. unprocessed and free from additives), organically grown vegetables, herb teas, fruit juices, mineral waters, dried fruits, non-meat sources of protein such as soy products (miso, tofu, soy chunks), nuts, live yogurt, honey and other spreads such as Marmite, peanut butter and tahini. They also do a flourishing business in food supplements and vitamins.

WHAT NOT TO EAT (AND DRINK)?

The above approaches, while differing sharply in some respects (notably over meat-eating), are broadly speaking in agreement that the following should be avoided:

> adulterated foods (i.e. containing preservatives, artificial flavouring, colourings, and so on), white sugar, white flour, cakes, sweets, chocolate, ice cream, animal fats, processed foods, soft drinks, coffee, alcohol.

FOOD ALLERGIES

To follow any one of the above systems slavishly is no substitute for bringing awareness into the choice of what one eats and being flexible according to changes in both one's internal energy process and environmental changes (for example, weather, work load).

We will assume that as far as possible the foods listed above as being definitely harmful have been eradicated from one's daily diet. The next step is to eat according to preference but with awareness, observing changes in one's mood and bodily well-being, high or low energy. If, for example, you feel unaccountably depressed or listless on awakening in the morning try to remember what you have eaten and drunk in the last day or so. It may well be that you have a food allergy and with a bit of detective work you should be able to isolate the offending substance.

The commonest food allergies relate to dairy products, grains (this includes beer and whisky), coffee and tobacco. In the USA an efficient and simple method of detecting food allergies has been developed which involves taking a blood sample and testing for allergy, drop by drop, to the 150 or so known allergens. In this country few such facilities as yet exist, though in his book *Not All in the Mind*, Dr Mackarness does outline a less convenient method involving a preliminary five-day fast on mineral water.

THE 'FEELING GOOD' DIET
Eat daily from among the following: cereals, pastas, whole grains (especially brown rice); wholewheat or rye bread; root vegetables (especially potatoes and carrots); green leafy vegetables (especially broccoli and spinach); salads (especially watercress); soy products; nuts, seeds, pulses (ie beans, peas, lentils); low fat dairy products (eg skimmed milk, cottage cheese); fresh or dried fruit free from additives. When cooking, steam or stir-fry vegetables in very little polyunsaturated vegetable oil or eat them raw with salad dressing. Use tamari instead of salt.

Eat occasionally for extra protein in winter:
fish (grilled, baked or steamed); poultry (make sure it is well cooked); eggs (preferably free range and not more than two or three in any one week).

Eat as rarely as possible:
meat (and not at all unless lean with fat trimmed off); fried foods; foods high in cholesterol (eg butter, hard cheeses, cream); sugar; salt.

Drink less caffeine and alcohol and more fruit juices (unsweetened), herb teas and mineral water. Use honey for sweetening.

The goal of the way of food is reached when you have become so sensitive and aware of your own needs that you naturally eat what the right things are *for you* — and this will be constantly varying. When you reach this stage you will experience an attraction for certain foods and a subtle aversion to others.

FOOD SUPPLEMENTS
You may need to take the following if you are
* ill or convalescent (vitamins C and E; pantothenic acid)
* on antibiotics (live yoghurt)
* suffering from pre-menstrual tension (vitamin B_6)
* a heavy drinker (vitamin B)
* a smoker (vitamin C)
* feeling irritable, anxious or suffering from insomnia (brewer's yeast; calcium)
* run down, lacking sexual energy (ginseng)

THE STRESS DIET
If you are eating wisely you should not need to take vitamin supplements. However, in times of stress Vitamins A, B and C are essential, together with a high-protein diet (especially liver), leafy green vegetables and wheat germ.

HOW TO EAT
Eating with awareness includes not only choosing food wisely but ensuring that it is well digested. The following suggestions are offered to ensure this:

1. Do not eat if you are upset, angry, feverish, or just before going to bed.
2. Give your attention to your food while you are eating. Listen to the conversation (if any), contribute if you wish, but all the while be *tasting* what you are putting into your mouth.
3. Chew food thoroughly before swallowing ('drink your food and eat your drinks'); digestion begins in the mouth.
4. If at all, drink sparingly until you have finished eating to avoid diluting the gastric juices.
5. Come away from the table feeling satisfied but not bloated.

INNER CLEANLINESS
The importance of cleansing the bowel of toxins has long been recognised in hatha yoga as essential for protecting the body against disease. Recent medical research has validated this ancient wisdom while (fortunately) advocating less drastic measures than those used by yogis. The NACNE and COMA

reports recommend increasing our fibre intake by about 25% from starchy foods like the following: bran, breakfast cereal, wholemeal bread, porridge, beans, vegetables, fruit.

ELIMINATION

The most common cause of feeling 'down' is a sluggish bowel or 'liverishness'. It is important to drink plenty of fluids, combined occasionally with a one-day or half-day fast. The latter may be a fruit-juice only or, especially good, a grape fast (about 4 lbs (2 kg) should last the day — eat the washed skins and some of the pips too). Any acute illness is best treated by a fast, and indeed it feels natural to us, as for animals, not to eat when ill. This way the body can devote its whole energy to ridding itself of toxins.

Cider vinegar (1 teaspoon) in warm water with honey is a great purifier taken first thing in the morning. If constipated, take live yogurt and prune juice rather than laxatives, add bran to your diet and practise massaging the abdomen (on an empty stomach) in a clockwise motion as well as the other abdominal massages described in a later chapter. Miso soup is excellent for the intestines (as well as being very nourishing) as are umeboshi plums. The latter are extremely salty and should be used sparingly whenever the digestive system is upset. Both miso (fermented soya-bean paste) and umeboshi plums are obtainable from most health food stores.

'BAD VIBRATIONS'

Other people and environments can be toxic to you as well as food, for we also assimilate finer, less tangible but nevertheless real forms of energy. Equivalents to junk food on this vibrational level can be aggressive, complaining or manipulative people, one-sided relationships, noisy or dirty surroundings and self-exposure to horrific, violent or sordid exploitation films. They are toxic to both mind and feelings, contaminating them with the projections, nightmares and negativity of others, which, if we absorb them, become part of the way we see the world.

We must learn to be more sensitive to what relationships and environments truly nourish us (i.e. leave us with a sense of lightness, satisfaction and expansion) and those which drain our energy, leaving us gloomy, contracted, irritable, guilty or paranoid. It is true that we get the experiences we deserve: there are no 'accidents'. We must therefore take responsibility for each situation, relationship and environment in which we choose to stay and ask ourselves the question: 'Am I getting anything out of this?' If not, change it — unless of course you 'get off' on being a martyr or scaring yourself. If unsure, cut through your tapes about how you should be responding to this person or situation by tuning into what you are actually experiencing in the way of body relaxation or tension and feelings of expansion or contraction. Trust your intuition, for at some level you *know*.

CLEANING THE AURA

Kirlian photography has proved the existence of the aura, the energy field that surrounds each of us as well as animals, plants and inanimate objects. If you are relaxed, open and looking with soft, unfocused eyes slightly *past* another person you may see it sometimes.

The aura changes colour, shape and brilliance according to our moods and state of health. It is possible to 'clean the aura' physically and thus feel clear, refreshed and purified at a deep and satisfying level. This indeed should be done regularly, especially when feeling drained after exposure to negative or scattered energy (for example working in noisy conditions, travelling in crowded trains, quarrels or interactions with depressive people).

It took me some time to discover the necessity for aura-cleaning after leading a cathartic group or massaging to restore my energy levels. The most natural way to do it is by taking a shower or a bath and drying briskly with a towel in the direction of the energy meridians (to be described in a later chapter). Be sure to include the head, as much energy from excessive thinking clings to the hair. Put on clean clothes afterwards. The refreshment and delicious sense of being clean again after bathing is probably more due to purifying our energy field than to washing sweat off our bodies. For an 'instant' aura-cleaning do the following routine:

1. Using the second and third fingers of both hands and pressing firmly on the 'third eye' between the eyebrows, trace a line up over the crown of the head down to the back of the neck and then down to the spine as far as you can reach. Still using the same fingers, pick up at the point you left off and continue pressing firmly down the spine (or rather slightly to each side of

it) and down the backs of the legs (simultaneously) to the calves. Shake each foot and kick off surplus energy.

2. Start again at the 'third eye', this time with the third and fourth fingers of the right hand. Trace firmly (without forcing) a line up and over the scalp and crown, down the back of the neck, along the left shoulder and the back of the left arm. Finish the movement with a sharp 'brush-off'.

3. Repeat the above, this time using the third and fourth fingers of the left hand and tracing the line over the head and down the back of the right arm.

4. Using the third and fourth fingers of both hands, trace the line up from the 'third eye' over the head to a point on the back of the neck between the ears. Here the hands separate, tracing two lines down the neck each side to join together again at the breastbone. Follow the centre line down the front of the body to the pubis. Both hands now simultaneously press firmly down the lines of the front of the legs, finishing with a 'brush-off' at the ankles.

5. Shake arms and hands a few times as if getting rid of drops of water, then shake all over to finish off.

This 'mechanical' aura-cleaning is good just before getting into bed at night and will promote deep, dreamless sleep. By 'mechanical' we mean cleaning the aura from the outside rather than by meditation. However, the process should not be done mechanically (i.e. without awareness and thinking about something else) but rather with the intention of leaving off the world's grime which has 'rubbed off' on one's psyche. As you perform this aura-cleaning, actually imagine that you are sloughing off an old and grimy skin and shaking yourself free of it.

CREATE A CONGENIAL LIVING ENVIRONMENT

As well as neutralizing bad or scattered vibrations, it is good to give attention to your own living environment. Just as when you know you look good you tend to feel good, so a clean and graceful living space will help to keep you positive. In fact, an effective way of changing your mood if feeling 'off' is to put energy into tidying up your living space. It works both ways, for how you live is an expression of where you are at. Make it unashamedly comfortable and as beautiful as you know how — for you as well as your friends. Let it be the place you like to be alone in, a place to relax with people you like, a place that feels good to you and them.

Colour and light therapy are now becoming an integrated part of medical work. If you have a say in re-decorating, remember that the most restful colours are green, blue and white. Red is disturbing to many people and black, depressing. Play around with lighting until you find the balance between harsh overhead glare and dim twilight that will give you eyestrain and cause your guests to bump into the furniture. Dimmer switches , once only seen in therapy rooms, are now in common use and excellently versatile for lighting meditation, togetherness or a rave-up.

Indoor plants will bring nature into your space and give you someone to nurture and talk to who will not answer back. Unless you have objections, cut flowers and incense can sweeten the vibrations, as can a picture or two of people or places you love. It's all a matter of taste — let it be *your* taste rather than passive acceptance of somebody else's.

GIVE YOURSELF SPACE

The essence of self-nourishment is 'giving yourself space'. By this is meant giving your own process the same respect and consideration that others expect and probably receive from you. Be sensitive to your rhythms, especially when you start to feel under pressure and overworked or merely need to be alone to rest or feel again who you are.

You may have chosen to work to earn a living but you are not on this earth to be a drudge or anybody's slave — unless, of course, if you want to be. Sometimes you will enjoy others' company, sometimes you will find them a drain on your energy. When that happens give yourself permission to withdraw gracefully — you don't have to be heavy, abrupt or rude.

If you are a workaholic, check out your priorities. Is this *really* the way you want to spend your life? However busy, allow a certain period of the day which is yours to spend with yourself: you may have to fight for it but it will be worth it.

BIORHYTHMS

Be aware, too, of the existence of your biorhythms, variations in your performance and mood which move in three basic energy cycles. Each cycle has an active phase where your energy will be high, a passive phase when it will be low and a changeover phase when your energy will be unstable. The cycles are:

The intellectual cycle, lasting thirty days, in which your concentration, judgement and ability to learn will be affected.
The emotional cycle, lasting twenty-eight days and affecting your moods and emotions.
The physical cycle, lasting twenty-three days and affecting stamina and body co-ordination.

These cycles can be predicted for each individual who can then understand why at times he or she seems 'full of energy' and at others depleted for no obvious reason. The Swiss, who produced the first biorhythm calculator in 1927, have used biorhythms in factories for safety (as have Japan and the USA), in hospitals for determining the best time for surgery, and in sport for selection of national gymnastic teams for high performance.

THE ART OF RELAXATION

Giving yourself adequate space to rest and relax is essential for your well-being. Without it you will be tense, fatigued, irritable and certainly not fun to be around. In addition you lay yourself open to mental and physical breakdown and probably a shorter life-span. You will neither look good nor feel good. Unfortunately, life in the West is so speedy that many find it hard to relax and some even to sleep. Yet relaxation is an art that can be learnt again. It is the knack of moving energy from the head back into the body. At first it has to be done gradually by gentle persuasion. Once you have the 'feel' of being totally in your body that is it; a blissful state of total relaxation that you can slip into at any time in any circumstances.

Basic Relaxation Exercise

Remove shoes and loosen clothing. Lie flat on your back, without a pillow, on a carpeted floor or a firm mattress. Legs should be slightly apart, arms by the side of thighs, palms up or down at will. Make yourself comfortable. Feel the floor under you and allow it to take over the job of supporting your weight. Take a few deep breaths, letting them out with a deep sigh. Tune in to the sounds around you, maybe a clock ticking beside your bed and street traffic outside. *Listening* is a great opener and relaxer, bringing you out of your private world of thoughts back into the real world. Have the intention that you are going to sink into yourself and for the present shelve all your responsibilities and worries. This moment is yours.

After a few minutes of listening to sounds, give attention to the weight of your body. Imagine it is sinking into the floor or mattress; feel it getting heavier and heavier. Feel the floor pressing upwards along the whole line of your body: heels, calves, buttocks, spine, shoulders, back of head. As your body gets heavier check where in your body you feel tight. First experience the tension, then silently give the command 'relax' and wait until it has been obeyed by that part of your body until you move on to the next. Be patient and gentle with yourself for you are learning new habits. Start with the left foot: toes, sole, ankle and then right foot: toes, sole, ankle. After the feet continue up the body in the following sequence, first allowing yourself to experience the tightness in each part, giving the silent command 'relax' and then waiting for the blissful sensation of expansion and heaviness to permeate that part before moving on to the next. After feet do:

    left calf
    right calf
    left thigh (front and back)
    right thigh (front and back)
    anus
    genitals
    small of back
    belly (spend a lot of time on this)
    shoulders
    whole back
    upper arms/lower arms/hands/fingers and thumbs
    eyes/forehead
    scalp
    jaw (let chin drop, lips apart)

We leave the jaw till last as it is almost impossible to relax it unless *you* are totally relaxed. There is so much tension in the face as this is part of your 'persona' and the mask with which you 'face the world', 'put up a good front' and keep a 'stiff upper-lip'. It is virtually the only part of your body that you present naked to the world and as the most expressive part of your body, it can betray your real feelings unless tightly controlled. Dropping the mask which serves to protect our vulnerability can feel quite threatening, so therapists usually leave working on it until the client has mobilized sufficient self-support to allow himself/herself to risk being transparent, 'visible'. Hence be especially patient with the jaw's tension. Likewise with the belly, for this is our centre, our 'guts' and the source of our very life-energy. In the next chapter, on bodyawareness, we shall be giving more attention to this most important part of the body.

Inevitably the mind will resist its loss of control over you as you surrender more and more to your body sensations. Don't fight it, when it clamours for attention ignore it and keep feeding more and more awareness to relaxing each part of your body in turn.

When you have finished, just lie quietly for as long as you wish, allowing the body to burden the floor/mattress and enjoying the bliss of total relaxation. If you do 'drop off' you will awaken, perhaps only after a few minutes, feeling as refreshed as after a good night's sleep. Indeed, this basic relaxation exercise should be practised by insomniacs, not only after going to bed but as often as possible.

Other aids to relaxation are:

Prarthana: Shoeless, with loose or no clothing, lie on your front, don't use a pillow; the face can be left or right cheek down at will. Place the instep of one foot over the sole of the other. Elbows pointing out, fold one hand over the other, palms down and place under your forehead so that the knuckle of the index or second finger of the upper hand presses gently against the 'third eye' between the eyebrows. Stay in this posture for as long as you wish. This ancient meditation posture is a 'mudra', a gesture of surrender which by its very nature induces deep relaxation almost immediately.

Tensing/Letting Go: This uses the gestalt principle of 'riding the horse the way it's going', and is described in the preceding chapter as a cathartic technique when overburdened or under pressure.

Relaxing Affirmations and Visualizations: Use affirmations, for example, 'I am totally relaxed', 'Life is good and I have all the time in the world', 'I am here to play and to enjoy myself', and so on, as described in Chapter One. It is important to believe and to *feel* the truth of your affirmation rather than to repeat it mechanically.

Sit or lie with eyes closed and visualize a sunny beach, garden or countryside in as much detail as you can. Make it as real as you can, modelling it on a place you know and have enjoyed. Linger there for a while, experiencing the colours, the fragrance of the flowers (or the sun-tan lotion!), the sounds of sea birds, the waves, children playing — or the peace of a secluded garden. Enjoy your creation for as long as you wish and come back refreshed after your brief holiday.

Another visualization that promotes relaxation is to imagine yourself expanding to fill first the room you are in, then the street, the town, the country, and so on. Go on expanding till you fill the earth, the solar system, the galaxy, and finally the universe. Stay expanded to the uttermost for as long as is comfortable then slowly, by the same stages in reverse, come back to the confines of your body. This expanding technique counteracts the contraction which is caused by tension and is the source of the discomfort. To avoid feeling disoriented by this 'spacy' exercise, ground yourself before going about your business by spending a few minutes feeling your own body from the inside, looking around the room, taking in furniture, pictures, curtains, and so on, and listening to sounds around you.

Present-Centredness: The above visualizations work to relax you because they entice the mind away from preoccupation with problem creating and solving (its main job) which make the body tense, to enjoyment and sensuality, which relax the body. The antidote to compulsive thinking, worrying, tension, nervousness and self-consciousness is, in Fritz Perls' words, to 'lose your mind and come to your senses'. Look around you at what is really there. Listen to the sounds of the real world, touch and smell objects, really taste whatever you happen to be eating or drinking, experiencing now — above all, feel, feel, feel.

This technique is particularly good for overcoming 'stage-fright', whether you have to talk in public or appear at a party where you know almost nobody. 'Taking in' the gathering and the ambiance with your eyes will neutralize *your* discomfort at being watched; really taking in what is being said with your ears will ease the tension arising from rehearsing what you should say next. To stay in the present is much more than a mere technique for relaxation: it is a counsel of perfection, the goal of spiritual paths as illustrated in sayings of Jesus and Buddha. The essence of meditation, present-centredness, will be discussed further in Chapter Six.

PLAY

Jesus said: 'Unless you become as little children you cannot enter the kingdom of heaven.' A relevant interpretation for us today might be: 'Unless you learn to stop taking life so seriously, to regain your sense of wonder, to be playful again, you will experience life as a problem to be solved rather than as a mystery to be enjoyed.' To practise relaxation techniques is fine but no substitute for a relaxed attitude to life. Take your time more, take more space and try to take life less seriously.

A nourishing life-style should make provision for opportunities to 'play' — whatever that means for you. Allow time for activities that are enjoyable purely for themselves and not goal-oriented. They could be sports, hobbies, theatre and cinema, travel, listening to or playing music, a night out at a restaurant or a disco, sex — whatever 'turns you on'. Enjoyment is the best therapy, for when you are enjoying you are truly living, relaxed, absorbed in the present, flowing with what is happening.

When you are enjoying something totally you come alive and feel good — all problems and tension disappear for the moment. Bring more of these moments into your life for quality, satisfaction — and fun.

4.

BODY AWARENESS

BODY-WISE

The body is your vehicle and to a large extent determines whether your ride through life is smooth or bumpy. It can be a joy-ride or a series of breakdowns and accidents. Like a car, it needs to be kept in good trim: regular servicing and grooming are essential. It needs the appropriate fuel to provide its energy and an efficient exhaust system. It prefers to be used lovingly rather than to be left stagnating in a garage.

There the analogy ends. Unlike a car, your body has a wisdom of its own and is often much wiser than you. It is your only real possession, in the sense that you do not lose it until death. It has its own sensitivity and awareness, which it is sharing with you all the time. Your oldest and closest friend, it sulks if you repay its untiring devotion to your real interests with neglect and 'ignorance' and may resort to drastic action to get your attention. This can be pain, illness, 'disease'.

That there is so much of the latter is an indication of how we are cut off from our bodies and indeed associate malfunctioning with love. As children we are filled with taboos about exploring our genitals; this we carry into later life as we block against sensuality if not genitality. At school we are encouraged to value acquisition of information above delight in the body's expressiveness. We bring the competitiveness of the examination room into our organized sports and even into the bedroom. When we are sick, our parents show more concern and caring than when we are overflowing with energy; we learn to use this to get out of unpleasant situations, especially school. These learned attitudes persist into adult life. At work some of us drive ourselves to exhaustion in the race for promotion; at home we find it impossible to relax.

All around us in our society we see the effects of this alienation from our own bodies: doctors' waiting rooms are filled night after night by people not so much sick as feeling needy and 'unwell' and expecting another 'prescription' to restore their well-being. Sex shops full of gadgets to sharpen jaded appetites; discotheques with deafeningly loud music to make some sort of impact on our insensitiveness; supermarkets selling instant meals for those not willing to give time and energy to eating fresh food.

BEING HERE NOW

The fact that we *have* a body does not necessarily mean that we are *in* that body. In fact most people are aware of their body only when it is either in pain or affording them pleasurable sensations, for example, when bathing, dancing or making love. *We* are where our attention is and usually it is, if focused at all, either out there in the material world or caught up in the inner fantasy world of 'memories, dreams and reflections'. Unless we are grounded and centred in the body we are too easily pulled off-centre by the energy around us and cut off from awareness of our own process and emerging needs by the mind-tripping in our heads. It is also to our advantage to become more sensitive, both for keener enjoyment of the senses and for early recognition of subtle messages of dis-ease.

The body-awareness exercises in this chapter are not 'keep-fit exercises' to be done mechanically but rather processes to be enjoyed with awareness for the aliveness, relaxation and heightened sense of oneself that they bring. We begin first with breathing for it is by shallow breathing that we desensitize ourselves and cut off experiencing what we are feeling. Also, changing your breath pattern changes your mood.

BREATHING TECHNIQUES

Exercise 1. Stand in a relaxed posture, feet shoulder-width apart. Breathe in as deeply as you can, raising your arms in front of you as you do so. Time it so that your arms are directly above your head as you complete the inhalation. Hold the breath for a count of five. Expel the air through the mouth in a deep sigh, allowing the arms to fall to either side and the shoulders to sag. 'Slump' — and relax totally. Repeat as often as feels right but do not force it. This exercise may also be done with the arms kept behind the back, hands joined together.

As you inhale, visulize that you are taking in nourishing positive energy in symbols that are meaningful to you (for example, health, freshness, purity, love, grace, life, God).

During the hold for a count of five, visualize this energy permeating your body, cleansing, healing and nourishing it.

As you exhale, visulize that you are expelling anything that is toxic in your life or a burden. Be specific (for example, sickness, self-destructiveness, worry).

Do this exercise whenever you feel you need 'room to breathe'.

Exercise 2. Close the right nostril with the right index finger. Breathe in deeply through the left nostril. Hold for count of three. Close left nostril with left index finger, removing right finger from right nostril. Count to three at end of exhalation. Still closing left nostril breathe in through the right nostril. Hold for count of three. Close right nostril with right index finger, releasing left nostril. Exhale slowly through left nostril. Count to three at end of exhalation. Repeat the sequence three times only. Yogic breathing ('pranayama') is extraordinarily powerful so do not overdo this exercise.

Good for balancing yin and yang energies and heightening calmness and clear thinking.

Exercise 3. Breathe in and out fast through the nose for as long as is comfortable. Once again, do not force yourself beyond your limits — you are not competing and there are no prizes. Omit this exercise if you suffer from heart, sinus, respiratory trouble or if you have a cold. Energizes and cleanses.

Exercise 4. Open the mouth and start to inhale and exhale, at first slowly and then in the rhythm that feels natural. As you breathe, focus your attention on the chest. As your feeling centre in the chest is energized you may start to feel sadness, anger or some other emotion. However, avoid expressing these and continue the breathing, thus permitting the energy to change into a finer form. Continue breathing as long as feels right. Stop if you feel dizzy or your fingers become numb — signs that you are hyperventilating. Energizes and sensitizes.

SLAPPING

Waken your sluggish body by 'slapping' it to life. Slap your arms, shoulders, sides, buttocks, thighs and calves. Tap your face, neck and scalp lightly and rapidly, using fingertips. This exercise is best done in the morning.

STRETCHING

Exercise 1. Begin breathing as described in Exercise 1 above. With arms above head, hold breath after inhalation and 'reach for the sky'. Then reach as high as you can with alternate arms, so that you can feel your sides being stretched. Complete as for breathing in Exercise 1 above with exhalations, sigh and slump.

Exercise 2. Clasp hands behind neck or head. Keeping chin up and elbows back, push your belly forward, leaning backwards as far as you can as you do so. Take a deep breath and exhale a few times in this position, then relax.

SHAKING

With feet shoulder-width apart, knees slightly bent, shoulders relaxed and arms hanging loose, start to shake your whole body, including head and hands. Imagine that you are shaking off all the tensions of the day and also any of your own negative feelings. At first *you* will be doing the movement but as you relax into the shaking your body will take over and shake the tension out of itself, an extraordinarily satisfying experience. Continue shaking for between 5 and 15 minutes, then lie down and rest quietly for 5 minutes.

This exercise is most useful on returning home after work or when tense or negative: since much negative energy is released, it is good to take a bath or a shower and put on fresh clothing. A real mood-changer, it will leave you feeling more relaxed and positive.

CENTERING

To be uncentered is to feel 'scattered', 'back on your heels' — uncomfortably vulnerable, needy or speedy, or simply unable to concentrate. To be centered is not to be thrown off balance easily by events and others' manifestations, to experience clarity and ability to initiate and focus, to respond rather than to react.

Exercise 1: Basic Centering

Stand with feet shoulder-width apart, toes pointing forward. Clasp hands, fingers intertwining, thumbs pointing forward. Raise arms (hands still clasped) in front and above the head as high as you can reach, keeping the heels on the floor and breathing in deeply through the nose. Holding the breath, bring clasped hands down to rest on the back of the neck and pause there for a count of two. Still holding the breath, return clasped hands to the highest point above the head and pause there for a count of two. Bring arms down to the side of the body, exhaling through the mouth. Rest, then repeat a few more times.

Exercise 2: 'The Tree'

Place the left heel in the right groin (or as high up on the right thigh as you can). Straighten the back and stretch your arms above your head (or clasp the hands behind the neck, elbows pushed back). Look straight ahead or slightly up with soft, unfocused eyes. If you start to wobble, imagine yourself to be a tree, stretching out branches to the sky and also deeply rooted in the earth. Hold this 'asana' (posture) for as long as feels comfortable. Don't strain. This tree's fruits? The sensation of centeredness you are getting in your body *now*. You are not practising for the future. Come out of the posture *slowly* and repeat, this time with the *right* heel on the *left* thigh.

Exercise 3: Pointing

With the left hand bring the left foot up behind you to touch the left buttock. Fix your gaze on an object slightly above eye-level and slightly to your right. Raise your right arm and point to the object with the right index finger, keeping the rest of the right hand relaxed and limp. Look along the right arm at the object. Breathe normally, relax into the posture, don't wobble. When it feels right, slowly come out of the posture and repeat it, this time bringing the right foot up to right buttock with right hand and pointing with the left.

Exercise 4: Looking

Sit in a relaxed way and just look around the room. To begin with, *feel* the atomosphere in the room: is it peaceful, noisy? Is it tidy or untidy? Start deliberately looking at furnishings and objects in the room, giving yourself enough time to really *see* each one as if for the first time, its size, colour, detail and so on. Carry on until you feel focused again, centered.

Exercise 5: 'What am I feeling?'
If you can, lie down and close your eyes. If not, withdraw and give yourself space to go inside yourself. Ask yourself: 'What am I feeling right now?' and try to experience it more clearly. You can do this in various ways: *tasting* the feeling (is it bitter or sweet?); visualizing its *colour* and *where* in the body you feel it most (for example, belly, heart, head); trying to give a *name* to the feeling (angry, fed-up, worried, tense, and so on). Try to identify the *exact* shade of feeling and do not be surprised when it changes into another feeling — keep zoning in on what *exactly* you are feeling. Do not identify and do not cathart, just be curious about where you are at.

GROUNDING
When we feel 'spacy', disoriented or simply 'out of touch' with what's happening around us, it is a sure sign that we need 'grounding', i.e. to be rooted more fully in our bodies. The body is the part of the environment closest to our being and to the extent that we are unaware of it, so our perception and experience of the rest of our environment will be vague or distorted. The following exercises will un-deaden our bodies, ground us and leave us feeling more 'connected' with the material plane.

Exercise 1: Toe wiggling
Just that. Wiggle them vigorously and enjoy it.

Exercise 2: Heel raising/lowering
Raise and lower your heels in a standing position. Give attention to the calf muscles, flexing and relaxing them as you do so.

Exercise 3: Tiptoeing
Walk round the room on the tips of your toes for as long as you can.

Exercise 4: Kicking
Walk around the room kicking the air vigorously from the knee. The movement has a 'snap' to it. Give attention to knees and thighs as you do so.

The purpose of the above rather bizarre exercises is simply to draw energy into the legs and feet by movement and attention. These are the parts of the body that connect the rest of you to the earth, and are furthest away from the head. To bring your awareness to legs and feet is a quick way out of the mind into relaxation and the experience of self-support.

Exercise 5: Squatting
Squat, keeping heels on the floor, toes pointing outwards, arms outstretched in front for balance, with hands either clasped or apart. Without moving your feet, rock your buttocks up and down.

Stand upright, relax, then repeat a few more times.

Exercise 6: 'Folded Leaf'
Repeat Exercise 5, but after rocking, instead of returning to a standing position, roll forward into a kneeling position with hands on floor in front of you. Lower the elbows to the floor outside the knees, level with and touching them. Bend over and lay your head gently between your hands. Alternately tense and relax belly muscles and anal sphincter. Do this several times, then just hold this 'folded leaf' position and relax into it. Do not hold your breath. This 'umbilical' posture can also be used purely for relaxation.

Exercise 7: The Cobra
From the 'folded leaf' posture move into a prone full-length position, elbows on the floor and palms face down on the floor, either side of your face, shoulder-width apart. Keeping palms, legs and feet in contact with the floor, press down on forearms to lever the torso up as far as is comfortable. Raise your head, look up, stretching the neck to see as high as you can. Let your chin drop so the mouth hangs open. Protrude the tongue loosely and try to look as idiotic as possible. Don't strain; there are no prizes for breaking your back or neck. Relax and repeat once more. This asana (hatha yoga posture) energizes the torso, spine, neck and face.

Exercise 8: Shoulderstand
This asana is good to do when too much stale energy is fixed in the lower part of the body, after standing or sitting for long periods.

Lie on the back, legs and feet together, arms by sides. *Slowly* draw both knees up. As your buttocks part company with the floor, support yourself on shoulders and upper back by pressing with hands on the floor and 'roll' into an inverted posture, legs together straight up in the air. Hold only briefly (not at all if you feel dizzy or experience dots before the eyes or buzzing in the ears) and *slowly* lower legs. Do only once at a session and, as with all yoga postures, only on an empty stomach. Lie still in the basic relaxation posture (described in the preceding chapter) for five minutes at least.

THE HARA

As well as feet and legs, the most vital area of your body from the point of view of grounding and centering is the belly. Situated just below the navel is your centre of gravity and source of primal energy. The Japanese call this point 'hara' (or 'tanden') and consider the man who has learnt to act from his hara as characterized by courage, decisiveness, serenity and stamina. He has 'guts', is 'gutsy'. To be grounded in the hara is to be balanced and earthy, confident, flowing, relaxed. It is central to the technique of tai-chi, the martial arts and zazen, and, not surprisingly, to the Japanese manner of suicide (hara-kiri). The following exercises will promote hara-awareness and put you in touch with your vital centre. Work on your hara only when the stomach is empty.

Hara Rubbing
Exercise 1: Stand, or lie on your back. With the right palm rub your belly briskly and firmly up and down from navel to pubis, focusing your attention on this area as you do so. Alternately tighten and relax the anus while continuing to rub the hara. Repeat with left palm, at least fifty times.

Exercise 2: Repeat the above exercise, this time, however, palming your whole belly *slowly* in a clockwise motion twenty times with the right hand.

Exercise 3: Stand in a lightly crouching position, knees bent, feet shoulder-width apart and toes pointing inwards. Hands may be resting lightly on the belly or thighs. Exhale completely. Before inhaling again, move the belly in and out several times by alternately contracting and relaxing the muscles of the solar plexus. Stop while you inhale and start the movements again after you have exhaled. Repeat the sequence several times.

Exercise 4: Bioenergetic Stress Position
Stand with feet shoulder-width apart, toes pointing slightly inward, knees slightly bent. Make fists and place them with knuckles in small of the back. Push your pelvis forward, lean backwards as far as you can, look up and raise your chin. The head should not be right back so that you are looking at the ceiling.

Open your mouth and let the chin hang loose so you look like an idiot (do not worry, nobody's watching!). Start breathing in and out through the mouth and imagine you are breathing into the belly, fuelling it with energy. As you breathe, lean back further, still with fists in the small of the back, mainly the same position of head, legs and feet. Try to find the 'stress position', a definite point where your body starts to vibrate and you can feel pleasure as energy is being released within the belly and pelvic region. Continue breathing for 3–4 minutes, then relax.

Exercise 5: Lie on your back, knees bent loosely, soles of the feet on the floor, shoulder-width apart, arms by the sides, palms downwards. Close your eyes, let the chin drop and through your open mouth start inhaling slowly and deeply and exhaling with a sigh. Focus your attention on your belly and genital area and imagine that you are breathing new energy into them and exhaling stale energy from them. Allow any feelings or thoughts to come up but don't feed them any more attention — just let them be there. Stop whenever you wish and relax.

'BIOENERGY'
The basic life energy of which the hara is the source (or more properly, the channel) is known as 'prana' in yoga and 'chi' in Taoist-oriented body disciplines (for example, acupuncture, tai-chi). Its pathways are exactly charted through meridians to be described in the next chapter and they are used in acupuncture to correct the energy imbalance which is considered to be the cause of illness. In the West it was given the name 'bioenergy' by Wilhelm Reich and a system called 'bioenergetics', developed by his successors, was designed to release this energy wherever it was trapped within the body by habitual muscular tension.

Dissolving these 'energy-blocks' can be accompanied by catharsis of emotions, past repression of which caused the first muscular 'holding' which is by now so familiar that we are no longer aware of it. The original feelings were repressed either through fear of punishment or because they threatened our self-image. They might be sexual feelings or anger or fear, primary emotions on the spontaneous expression of which there are heavy taboos in our society. Reich's views on the effects of social conditioning brought down the wrath of the custodians of the *status quo* — a fate suffered so often by pioneers of emancipation. That such emancipation is needed is evidenced by the flourishing market for stories and films of sex, violence and horror.

PLEASURING

One of the heaviest taboos we were subjected to as children was against pleasing and pleasuring ourselves. 'Be a good boy/girl' meant, in fact, 'If you do what *you* want to do, you are bad'. For many adults, being 'self-centred' is equated with being insensitive and uncaring to others, not necessarily true at all for a mature individual. Similarly, many people have a resistance to experiencing pleasure in their bodies. As children most of us courted displeasure from significant adults if we 'turned ourselves on' by playing with our (or anyone else's) genitals. We got a lot of attention and concern when we were having a bad time with illness, bumps and bruises or nightmares, but not when we were pleasuring ourselves. Expect therefore to feel resistance to the pleasurable feelings that arise in the belly and genitals as you relax into the body.

Do not automatically assume that all bodily pleasure is genital or even that if you start to feel sexy, you have to do anything about it. Similarly with anxiety, anger or other 'stuff' that might arise, especially with bioenergetic exercises 4 and 5: accept them but do not feed them attention or cathart. Allow the satisfying bodily sensations to grow, and enjoy them.

EXERCISE

'Energy is delight,' said William Blake. There are few more delightful ways of both inviting and expressing this overflowing life in you than exercising the body. Exercise is healthy, relaxing and fun. Sports, swimming, running, jogging, walking do you good and make you feel good. Dancing is exercise too and a great energy raiser. Thus if you never even try any of the techniques described in this book and yet dance freely and joyously, you will be on the right track. (You could even skip the cathartic techniques in Chapter Two and dance away your anger, frustration or despair — it's the same energy!)

As a technique for enhancing body awareness, dancing is ideal, for in order to be able to dance in rhythm one has to be centered, grounded and listen to the music. Dance when alone, to any music you can *feel*. Or dance in public. Here you may encounter your conditioning in the form of self-consciousness (a misnomer for inhibition) before really 'getting into it' or even before venturing on to the disco floor.

'Self-consciousness' arises from misdirected attention: it is a self-contraction induced by the twin ideas that you are being critically observed by others and that you are not OK as you are. Neutralize these 'terrible twins' by feeling the support provided by your legs and feet and by centering your attention in the hara. At the same time check out if anyone really is watching you. If they are, tell yourself that they are in fact *admiring* you — and dance! Do not dance mechanically; be inventive, expressive and total. Use and enjoy your whole body

5.

SELF-MASSAGE

TOUCHING YOURSELF FOR HEALTH

Self-massage helps to ground us in the body as well as being pleasurable, prophylactic and healing. Massage tones muscles, removes toxins, stimulates the circulation, promotes vitality and relaxation. To massage one's own body is very natural — we do it all the time to help ourselves feel better. We scratch our heads when perplexed, press bumps and bruises, rub our hands in satisfaction or wring them in despair. We associate touching with the transfer of positive, loving energy from the laying-on of hands of the faith-healer, the caresses of lovers or the hugging of a hurt or frightened child by its mother.

Even apparently purely clinical touching by physicians or nurses may have a soothing effect on patients simply because they know they are now under expert care. To touch someone means: 'I care for you.' Conversely we 'keep our distance' from people we *don't* care for: indeed, if they disgust us we 'wouldn't touch them with a barge-pole'.

Relaxing, energizing and pleasuring your own body by self-massage is therefore also your own validation of it as acceptable and lovable and a powerful neutralizer of any negative 'trips' you might have about it being too fat, skinny, or otherwise not measuring up to the current sexy stereotypes of the commercials and advertisements.

DO'S AND DON'TS

DO:

    (i) make sure the room is warm enough before you start to massage so you don't get a chill, especially when relaxing afterwards.

    (ii) have the intention that you are going to give loving energy to the body that is your present home.

(iii) feel what you are doing and listen internally for any messages as to what your body wants from you next. These may be felt as an itch, tension or fatigue in a certain muscle, or special pleasuring from a particular stroke. Go with your own process rather than slavishly sticking to a routine sequence of strokes.

(iv) enjoy yourself.

DON'T:

(i) massage until at least one-and-a-half hours after a meal - longer if it's been a heavy one.

(ii) massage over scar tissue or varicose veins, or if you are feverish, unwell or pregnant.

(iii) overdo it — stop each stroke *before* you start feeling drained.

(iv) bath or shower afterwards — better to bathe before.

BASIC SELF-MASSAGE

The following routine takes 10–15 minutes and forms an invigorating start to the day or a relaxing session after you have 'come down' from travelling home after work and have showered or bathed. Repeat each stroke for as long as feels good.

Belly palming

Do this first to bring back your body awareness after sleeping or being 'out there'. Palm the belly firmly in a clockwise motion. Briskly rub the area vertically between navel and pubis as described in the 'hara rubbing' exercise in Chapter Four.

Scalp tapping

Apply friction to the scalp using the fingertips, rubbing and tapping. Be gentle.

Neck squeezing

Interlock the fingers behind the neck and squeeze with the palms. Relax, then squeeze again. Repeat.

Eye palming

Place palms over the eyes. Have the fingers crossed over the forehead but do not press on the eye itself. Close the eyes and relax. Hold for as long as you have time.

Face massage

Rub the hands together vigorously to warm them, then place them on the face, fingers over the eyes. Do this several times. Rub the palms briskly up and down the cheeks. Smooth the forehead firmly using the two middle fingers of both hands simultaneously. Start the strokes from the middle of the forehead and end at the temples. Include the 'frown lines'.

Tap the whole surface of the face, lightly using the fingertips. Applying firm pressure and using the second fingers simultaneously, trace the line of the upper jaw from each side of the nostrils down to the sides of the mouth.

Place second and third fingers on each jaw and clench the latter. Shift the position of the fingers, if necessary, so that they are right over the tensed jaw muscle. Relax the jaw and rub as hard as is comfortable, using small circular strokes.

Pull weird faces, moving the mouth as if made of rubber.

Arm meridian massage

With the right hand rub the whole length of the left arm from the back of the left hand to the left shoulder, then down the left forearm to the palm of the left hand. Use brisk strokes, applying firm, constant pressure. Repeat half-a-dozen times.

Repeat the sequence on the left arm, using the right hand. This sequence follows the flow of 'chi' energy along the meridians (described later in this chapter) and heightens vitality. Massaging against the meridian flow (i.e. *down* the outside of the arm and back *up* the forearm to the biceps) serves to lessen the energy flow and can be used if one is too 'speedy' and scattered before retiring at night or settling down to work demanding concentration.

Leg meridian massage

Similarly the leg meridians may be massaged, either to stimulate or lessen the energy flow. Both legs may be massaged simultaneously, left hand for the left leg, right hand for right leg. The meridian direction is the opposite of that for the arms, i.e. *down* the outside leg from hips to ankles and up the inside leg to the upper inside thighs.

Back massage

Squeeze the left trapezius (shoulder muscle) with the fingers of the right hand and vice versa. Make fists and *gently* pummel and rub the lumbar region. Do not use the knuckles.

Hand massage

Rub the hands vigorously together. Pull each finger from base to tip, using the thumb and index fingers of the opposite hand, finishing the stroke with a snap. Grasp one hand with the other in any way that feels good and squeeze it firmly with a stroking motion. Alternate with each hand. Use the thumb to smooth the palm of the other hand.

Foot massage

Ideal when fatigued or for relaxation. Sit in any comfortable position which allows massage of the sole of each foot in turn. Make a fist and press the knuckles hard into the ball of each foot, using a 'screwing' motion. Do the same with the instep. Make a ring with thumb and index finger, insert each toe in turn through it and pull firmly with a wriggling stroke. Pinch the tip of each toe. Rub the index finger between each toe — a deliciously sensual experience for most people.

Using the second fingers, smooth the hollows on each side of the achilles tendon in a downward direction. Pinch the heel a few times sharply. Finish with grasping one foot with both hands from the sides, thumbs overlapping toes. Press with the fingers into the sole, meanwhile smoothing the top of the foot forward with the fleshy part of each palm. Repeat with the other foot.

ZONE THERAPY (REFLEXOLOGY)

If you have time, give longer to massaging hands and feet, for by doing so you will be stimulating the internal organs and increasing circulation to all areas of the body. It is not clear why this should be so. The important thing for us is that this zone therapy (or reflexology) *does* work, probably via the nerve endings in hands and feet connecting with the internal organs. Since the hands and feet are the parts of the body with least depth to them, these nerve endings lend themselves easily to manipulation. The approximate position of these nerve endings and the parts energized by their manipulation have been charted. They are given in the maps of hands and feet reproduced on pages 63 and 64.

The exact reflex area for each organ may vary slightly from person to person. Note that the reflex areas on the left hand and

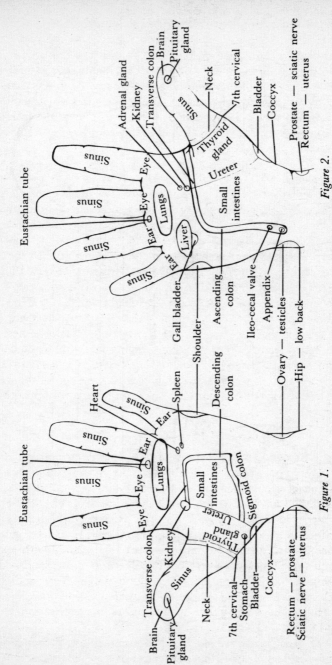

Figure 1.

LEFT HAND — PALM UP

Figure 2.

RIGHT HAND — PALM UP

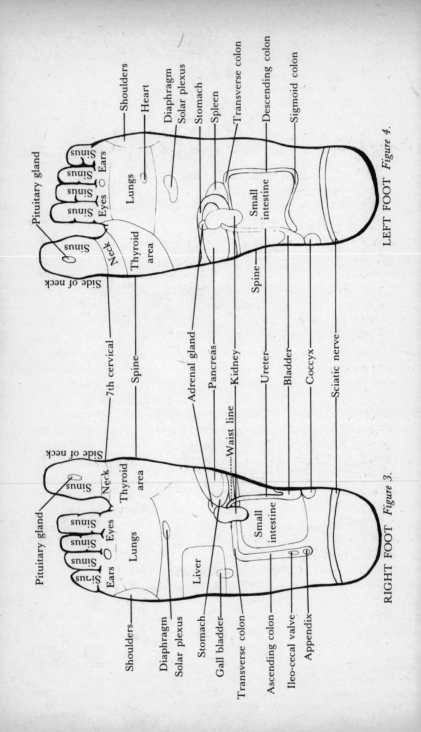

RIGHT FOOT *Figure 3.*

LEFT FOOT *Figure 4.*

Pituitary gland
Sinus
Sinus
Sinus
Sinus
Sinus
Eyes
Ears
Neck
Side of neck
Shoulders
Diaphragm
Solar plexus
Stomach
Gall bladder
Transverse colon
Ascending colon
Ileo-cecal valve
Appendix
Thyroid area
Lungs
Liver
Small intestine

7th cervical
Spine
Adrenal gland
Pancreas
Kidney
Waist line
Ureter
Bladder
Coccyx
Sciatic nerve

Pituitary gland
Sinus
Sinus
Sinus
Sinus
Sinus
Eyes
Ears
Neck
Side of neck
Shoulders
Heart
Diaphragm
Solar plexus
Stomach
Spleen
Transverse colon
Descending colon
Sigmoid colon
Thyroid area
Lungs
Small intestine
Spine

left foot correspond to organs on the left side of the body, and vice versa. Twin organs (for example, kidneys, lungs) have two corresponding reflex areas, one on each hand and foot. Organs overlapping both sides (for example, colon) will overlap each foot and hand. The upper half of the body has reflex areas on the upper parts of the foot and vice versa.

We use these maps in reflexology both for diagnosis and for healing. When massaging the feet note any areas which are painful or tender or in which you can feel small gravel-like nodules. Any of these is a sign that all is not well and by referring to the map of the foot the affected organ can be identified. Don't panic! It does not mean that you are necessarily ill, simply that the organ is functioning under par. However, you have advance warning and you would be foolish to ignore it. Massage the area firmly, using thumb pressure and knuckles to crush any crystalline deposits. The more painful foot massage is, the worse shape you are in, so persevere through the pain to send nourishing energy to the depleted organ. On the other hand, do not be too rough on your feet or in too much of a hurry. After your first reflexology massage allow a couple of days, rest for the body to absorb the toxins released into the bloodstream. You may feel dizzy or nauseous but this will pass.

Having massaged an organ in distress, help it in other ways. For example, if your liver reflex area (on the side of the ball of the right foot) is painful or tender, as well as massaging the liver reflex area avoid fried or fatty foods, alcohol, drugs and other things that give your liver a bad time. Similarly if your lung reflex area is tender, as well as massaging this area you may need to cut down or give up smoking as well as cutting out mucus-producing dairy products. A caution is in place here. Treat reflexology as a tool, not as a panacea. If you are obviously ill or in pain, consult a qualified medical practitioner. Do not get obsessed with looking for signs of incipient disease. Used with awareness and common sense, reflexology can be an aid to keeping your body in 'tone' so that illness does not have a chance to develop.

BATES EYE EXERCISES

Though not, strictly speaking, massage, the Bates method of improving eyesight can be incorporated into the self-massage routine. We have already included the eye-palming exercise, one of the most effective ways of relaxing the eyes for better vision. Another exercise with the same effect is called 'swinging'. Standing in a relaxed position, gently sway the whole body from side to side as if you were a pendulum, raising each heel (not the whole foot) alternately. Continue for five to ten minutes. Keep eyes soft and unfocused, open for a minute then closed for a minute, open again, then closed, and so on. Every now and then blink them as you swing. In fact blinking, together with palming and swinging, is the third method in the Bates system of inducing eye relaxation. We should learn to blink (effortlessly) once or twice every ten seconds during the course of the day.

ACUPRESSURE

Some of the massage techniques described above are used in shiatsu, the ancient Japanese art of acupressure. Literally, 'shiatsu' means 'finger pressure' and the latter is employed on points throughout the body to eliminate fatigue, prevent the development of sickness, and to stimulate the body's natural ability to heal itself. Acupressure can relieve pain and tension, and, skilfully used, can be successful in treating a wide range of complaints from headaches, haemorrhoids and arthritis to impotence and frigidity.

Acupressure uses the same points as acupuncture on the energy channels throughout the body called meridians. Unlike acupuncture, however, fingers and thumbs (and sometimes fists) are used instead of needles. For example, when we massage the face we are stimulating many meridians at once: rubbing the cheeks massages the stomach and small intestine meridians, while scalp-tapping works on the bladder, gall-bladder and triple heater meridians.

THE MERIDIANS

The fourteen meridians are the pathways along which 'chi' or bioenergy flows through the body. They were first recorded some four thousand years ago in China, based on centuries of empirical observation. Each meridian is named from the organ or function served in the course of its path. Thus we have the following meridians:

lung
large intestine

stomach
'spleen' (pancreas)
heart
small intestine
bladder
kidney
'heart constrictor' (circulation)
'triple heater' (body temperature)
gall bladder
liver
'governing vessel' ⎫ regulators of
⎬   other
'conception vessel' ⎭ meridians

These meridians are divided into positive and negative (yang and yin). Yang meridians start from the head, face and fingers and finish in the feet or centre of the body. Yin meridians are the other way round. There are three yang and three yin meridians in the arms, and three of each in the legs. The 'governing vessel' meridian extends up over the middle of the face and down the back while the 'conception vessel' runs from the mouth to the genitals. The six yang meridians are large intestine, stomach, small intestine, bladder, triple heater and gall bladder. The six yin meridians are lung, spleen, kidney, heart, heart constrictor and liver.

MERIDIAN MASSAGE AND MEDITATION
As long as bioenergy flows smoothly along the meridians we experience well-being. If, for whatever reason, its flow is unsynchronized we feel 'off' and may eventually develop overt symptoms of dis-ease. If we develop our awareness to the point where we are very sensitive to these subtle changes in our body energy it is possible to harmonize the bioenergy flow again by feeling the path of each meridian in turn. This can be done first using the thumb or tips of the index and middle fingers, massaging the meridians along their length in the direction of the bioenergy flow. Meridians 1–12 should be thus massaged in the order in which they have been listed above.

As you become familiar with the meridians and the 'feel' of your own bioenergy you can practise 'meridian meditation'. Sit in a relaxed but alert posture, either on a cushion or a chair, keeping the back straight without straining. Eyes should be closed and hands on the knees.

Starting with the lung meridian, trace in your mind its pathway and visualize the energy coursing along its route. Do this with each meridian in turn. Know that where you have difficulty in continuing along a pathway there is a blockage, either in your concentration or in that meridian. In either case it is good to persist in feeding attention (i.e. energy) to the spot. If necessary, keep returning to that meridian at intervals during the day, until you can 'see your way through'. Know then that you have probably averted incipient illness in its embryonic stage, for dis-ease can only manifest in your body if the energy is blocking or not flowing evenly along the meridians.

ACUPRESSURE POINTS

Meridian meditation has been practised in Taoism for thousands of years. It was recommended for longevity to his disciples by the sage Lao-Tzu, who was, we are told, at least 160 years old when he died. Meridian meditation needs much practice to acquire the requisite sensitivity to be able to detect subtle energy-changes along the meridians. Acupressure on the other hand is immediately effective.

Acupressure points are interconnections or stops along the meridians where blocked bioenergy tends to stagnate. They respond straightaway to pressure, to correct and adjust energy flow. This pressure is applied firmly with thumb, fingertip or knuckle, moving the skin briskly in a counter-clockwise direction for about twenty seconds. The acupressure points are tiny and need to be located exactly before pressing. The illustrations give the approximate location only. Probe deeply in that area until you feel a definite sensitivity or twinge. This is the point on which to continue pressure in the manner described.

Acupressure acts straightaway to bring relief from pain, unpleasant symptoms or feelings such as those listed in Figures 5 and 6 with the corresponding acupoints. Bear in mind that it offers a preferable alternative to aspirins, tranquillizers or patent medicines and is a sort of 'first aid'. It is no substitute for professional attention from your doctor or dentist if symptoms persist or you are worried about your health.

ACUPRESSURE POINTS

1 Asthma
2 Neuralgia
3 Impotence
4 Dental work — toothache
5 Colds — sinus congestions
6 Claustrophobia
7 Anxiety — depression

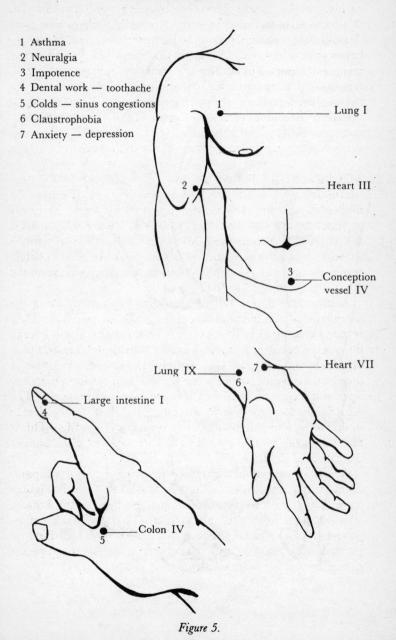

Figure 5.

ACUPRESSURE POINTS

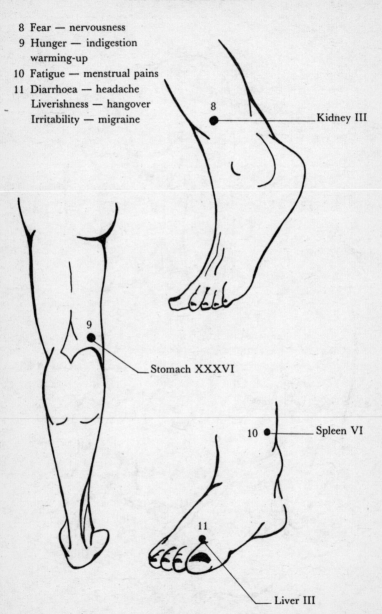

8 Fear — nervousness
9 Hunger — indigestion
   warming-up
10 Fatigue — menstrual pains
11 Diarrhoea — headache
   Liverishness — hangover
   Irritability — migraine

8 ——— Kidney III

9 ——— Stomach XXXVI

10 ——— Spleen VI

11 ——— Liver III

Figure 6.

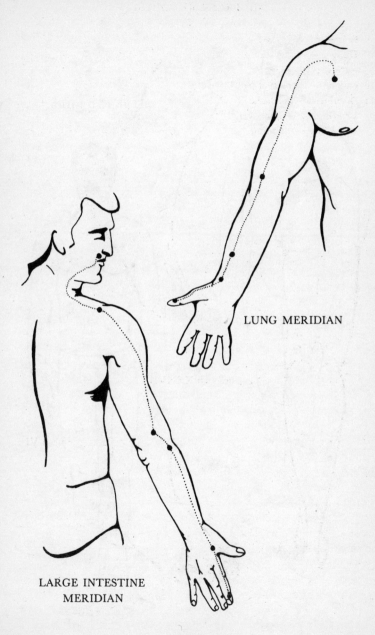

LUNG MERIDIAN

LARGE INTESTINE
MERIDIAN

Figure 7.

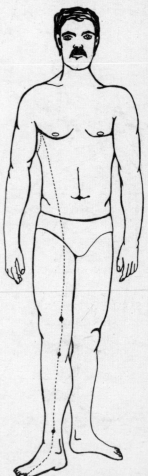

SPLEEN MERIDIAN

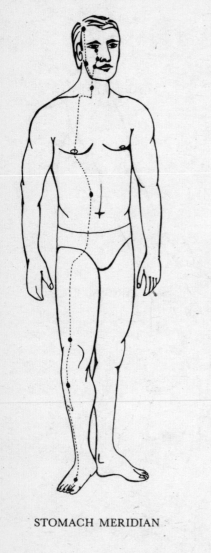

STOMACH MERIDIAN

Figure 8.

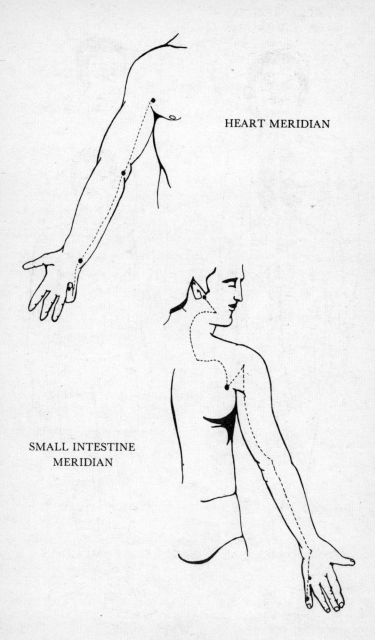

HEART MERIDIAN

SMALL INTESTINE
MERIDIAN

Figure 9.

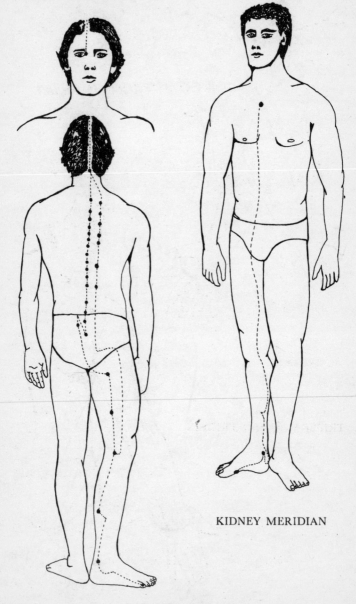

BLADDER MERIDIAN
BACK AND FRONT

KIDNEY MERIDIAN

Figure 10

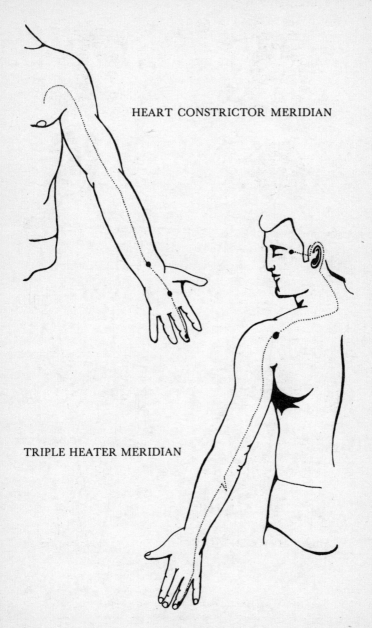

HEART CONSTRICTOR MERIDIAN

TRIPLE HEATER MERIDIAN

Figure 11.

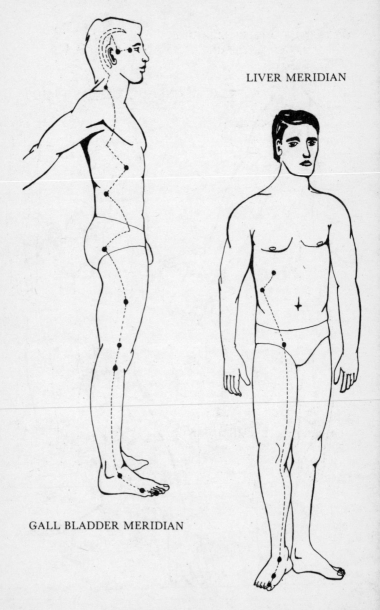

LIVER MERIDIAN

GALL BLADDER MERIDIAN

Figure 12.

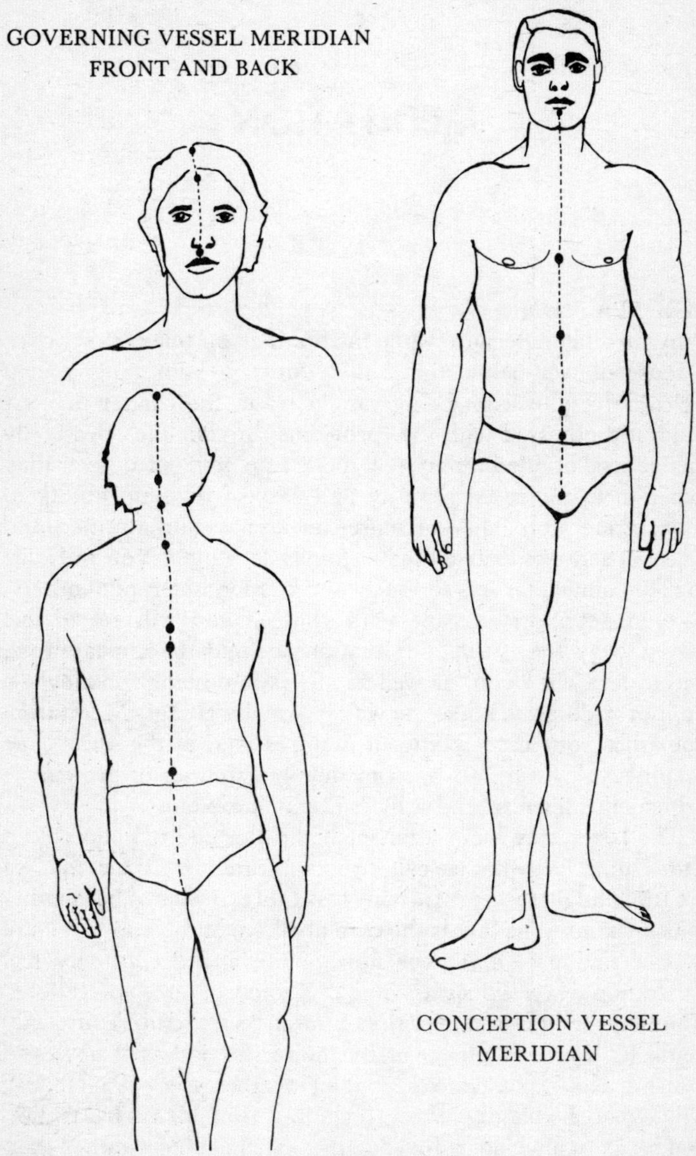

GOVERNING VESSEL MERIDIAN
FRONT AND BACK

CONCEPTION VESSEL
MERIDIAN

Figure 13.

6.

MEDITATION

MEDITATION

Why meditate? Because while meditating you relax, experience
a sense of well-being and centeredness in your body and a
welcome respite from being caught up in the chatter in your
head and obsessed with the 'problems' in your life. Gradually
the effects of meditation will permeate into your everyday
experience: increased serenity and ease of relating, ability to
concentrate more, sharper senses, awareness and intuition and
a deeper sense of yourself that is totally satisfying. You will start
to take yourself far less seriously and be more tolerant of others.
As you get more in tune with yourself you will get to feel
instinctively the 'truth' of situations behind the appearances,
and to feel when you, as well as others, are being 'phoney' —
i.e. not 'riding the horse the way it is really going'. Meditation
nourishes your inner being; it matures you, at the same time
keeping you fresh and open to new possibilities of growth. It
brings effortlessness and a life without 'problems'.

The latter may seem a far-fetched claim and too good to be
true. But in fact what we call 'problems' are merely *facts* that we
are unwilling to accept. It is our resistance to what is happening
to us or around us that is the core of all our 'problems'. We are
in fact saying 'No' to the flow of life and accordingly feel
frustration when it does its thing regardless of our expectations.
The non-meditator experiences himself as a victim, constantly
being let down by others or by the bitch-goddess 'Luck' and
fighting a losing battle to 'keep it all together' the way it 'should
be'. He or she blames others (including God) for his frustration
and seeks to alleviate it by changing circumstances rather than
attitudes. His existential statement is: 'If *things* were different I
would be happy.' That of the meditator is: 'If *I* were different I

would be blissful all the time.' For the meditator comes to realize that he is never a victim but, on the contrary, the source of his own creations. He is therefore not so much interested in *solving* his problems as in *dis-solving* them by becoming more aware of the problem-creating machine within him that we call 'mind'. Before you can switch off a machine you first have to find the switch.

For our minds are indeed machines, or, more exactly, computers. Meditation will not impede your capacity to concentrate, memorize, calculate or plan: on the contrary, the fact that it improves your performance in these proper functions of the mind is a reason why TM has been 'adopted' by big business corporations in the USA. Meditation will, however, make you aware of the programmes that you have in the past accepted, or yourself fed into your mind-computer. We take them for granted, simply because we are so familiar with them, and mistake them for irreversible and eternal truths.

To attempt to move in a fast changing world with these rigid programmes from the past is to invite collision as surely as if we were driving a car while looking only in the rear mirror. Or, to change the image, it is as if we try to see the real world through spectacles that have a representation of the world painted on the *inside* of the lenses. Meditation brings awareness of our self-defeating, self-destructive patterns and we begin to suspect the existence of an objective world beyond our painted specs. When this happens we are on the path to what in the East is called 'enlightenment' or liberation from our own illusions.

These programmes of the mind we call the ego, which is therefore wider than the mere selfishness or pride that the word commonly means. Together (though not at all in harmony with each other) they are behind the way we see the world and present ourselves in it. They are the result of past experiences and conditioning and include:

> opinions
> judgements
> ambitions
> desires
> memories
> ideals
> fears
> likes/dislikes
> projections and so on.

'But these are natural, only human,' I hear you saying. True: it is OK (in the sense that you will not suffer) to have them so long as you are willing to modify them or relinquish them when they are no longer realistic or life-supporting.

'Identification' said Gurdjieff, 'is the only sin.' Such identification, for example, with a self-image of success or prosperity, could lead to suicide if your company goes bust. Clinging to memories, brooding over unrealized ambitions, obsessional fears — all can drive you crazy. Insight into this connection between attachment to getting our own way and suffering was the path of the Buddha to inner peace (nirvana) and is as relevant for us today as it was for him. Awareness heals, and once you have seen, or more exactly, *felt*, the connection between cause and effect ('karma') in what you do, say or think, next time round you will not repeat it so mechanically. It is hard to put your hand in the same fire twice, assuming it even occurs to you to do so.

Those who 'got wise' to the mind and its devilish tricks have shown us ways to make it a good servant rather than a poor master. According to their different temperaments and insight, these Masters emphasize certain paths and techniques. But they all point in the same direction to that 'knowing', peace and bliss that lies beyond the compulsive thinking, conflicts and attachments that we call 'mind'. To attain this enviable state permanently is not cheap and not perhaps for everybody. By persevering with any of the meditation techniques described below that you enjoy, however, you could for once taste the relief that comes from not taking seriously every thought or feeling that comes to you and you might even get a glimpse of what in zen is called 'no-mind'.

You will, hopefully, come away from a meditation session feeling refreshed, clearer, more centered and grounded in your body as you 'lose your mind and come to your senses'.

DISIDENTIFICATION EXERCISE

This exercise can be practised on its own or before any of the 'witnessing' meditations such as vipassana or zazen.

Do the basic relaxation exercise described in Chapter Three. Afterwards repeat to yourself slowly the following words, stopping after each sentence to allow what you have just said to sink in. Stress the words underlined.

'I am *not* my body. I *have* a body and can *feel* it. Therefore *I* am not my body. (pause)

'I have *feelings*. Sometimes they are pleasant, sometimes unpleasant. They come and go within me. I *can* feel them, therefore *I* am separate from my feelings. (pause)

'I have *thoughts*. They arise in my consciousness, then disappear again. I can *observe* these thoughts as they come and go. Therefore I am not my *thoughts*.' (pause)

If you feel you didn't 'connect' with what you were saying, repeat the words again. Afterwards just lie quietly and experience what sensations you are getting in your body, how you are feeling and all the thought processes that are going on in your head. Know that you are this experiencer, not the experience.

MEDITATION POSTURE

The traditional postures for meditation are sitting or kneeling. Whichever you choose, make sure you are *comfortable*: you don't *have* to torture yourself to get enlightened, in fact just the reverse. Keep your spine erect without straining and your eyes either closed or half-open, looking slightly downwards, unfocused, and soft. By 'soft' is meant 'don't glare'. You are not trying to see anything 'out there'. In fact you are withdrawing your attention from preoccupation with the busy world outside and 'turning in'.

If you can sit cross-legged do so, supporting your buttocks on a firm cushion and your knees on the floor. If this is excruciating, try a chair, but sit on it in such a way that your feet are on the floor and your back is straight and unsupported. Hands should be joined, either the back of the left hand resting on the palm of the right, which in turn rests on the pubis (vipassana) or finger and thumb tips of both hands lightly touching each other to form an 'O' (zazen).

If kneeling, support the buttocks on the heels and remember not to let your shoulders sag. The feeling you are trying to encourage by adopting a meditation posture is that of total relaxation in your body accompanied by unforced alertness. It is like being asleep and conscious at the same time, reversing our normal state of being hyperactive and dreamy. The compact, still posture avoids leakage of energy, thus allowing it to accumulate; the erect spine stops you falling asleep and the knees, soles or insteps on the floor ground you.

WITNESSING

The purest form of meditation is witnessing, for when you are just a witness you are being your true self, stripped of ego-identifications; pure consciousness, subjectivity, a nameless 'I'. Witnessing is really jumping in at the deep end, for we are so accustomed to being absorbed in our own process or caught up with what's happening around us that such detachment, 'taking no notice' of thoughts, feelings, sensations and sense-impressions, does not come easily.

Too often we will forget our rôle of the impartial aloof witness, the 'fool on the hill', and be drawn down the well-trodden dirt-track of compulsive thinking by thoughts or feelings particularly charged with energy. Be patient and return to witnessing again. New habits are rarely learned overnight. The more relaxed the body and less active the mind, the less the pull to 'do' or think and of course the easier it is to witness. For this reason, enlightened Masters have always devised meditation techniques to facilitate detachment for their disciples.

Buddhist meditations give the mind toys to play with, just as a parent might encourage a fractious child to get absorbed in drawing or a game so that he is not clamouring for attention, so that the parent may have some space for himself. For this is what you are really doing when you meditate, merely taking space for yourself to relax a while, not to dream or fall asleep, but to experience your own being, limitless, silent, empty and yet full of peace and bliss.

VIPASSANA (WITNESSING)

The 'toy' in this Buddhist meditation is watching the rise and fall of the breath. 'Vipassana' in fact means 'breath' and while the mind is (we hope) happily engaged in this perfectly useless activity, it cannot come up with any distractions. This is because it can only give attention to one thing at a time. Just breathe gently and normally, through the nose and be aware of your breathing all the time. Don't *concentrate* on it; just be aware that it is happening.

Concentration is a focusing of attention on a particular spot for some objective. Meditation is more passive, allowing what is to be there as it is without judgements, interpretations or mind-trips whatever, including 'getting something out of it' — or allowing all this stuff to be there too if that is what is happening right now. Attach no importance to *what* you are witnessing: the point is to get accustomed to the feel of *being* a witness.

ZAZEN (SITTING)

Zazen means 'just sitting'. It is the basic meditation of Zen Buddhists for whom the path to enlightenment is everyday life lived with awareness and totality. There is a Zen story of two disciples of different Masters who were each trying to convince a crowd of bystanders of their Master's greatness. '*My* Master,' one disciple proudly declared, 'can walk across the river to the other side. How about that!'

To this the other retorted, 'Is that all? Mine works even greater miracles, for when he eats he just eats and when he sits he just sits.' By this 'just' is meant the pure action uncontaminated by mind-trips, doing what you're doing without, for example, thinking about something else or perhaps wishing you weren't doing it at all. Discursive thinking is a hole in the bucket of your awareness: it is a leakage of attention/energy which results subjectively in less sharpness and intensity of experience of what you are doing.

Like all meditations, zazen is a device to wake us up out of our robot-like mechanicalness, so that we can again experience the immediacy and freshness of ordinary life, as we did as children. The device here is just to sit and allow whatever happens to happen. The tigers of the mind will soon appear to try to distract you from doing something totally for a change. Flashbacks from the past and worries about the future will try to hypnotize you out of fully experiencing this moment. Don't fight them for they are paper tigers and your attention will only feed them energy and make them more real. Rather, intend to experience how it feels to sit there *whatever* happens, including even earthquakes.

Do not regard noise as a distraction, include it as part of your unique present experience of sitting. If your mind is particularly rebellious, then give it toys to play with, for example, concentrating on the hara, counting to ten on each exhalation and repeating as necessary or pondering the question 'Who am I?' 'Sit it out', and gradually you will come to see that you are not the mind and can ignore its monkey chatter at will.

'WHO AM I?'

In the Rinzai school of Zen the Master sets the disciple a 'koan', a riddle for his mind to get its teeth into. However, since the riddle is nonsense, (for example, 'What is the sound of one hand clapping?'), the mind soon finds that it has bitten off more than it can chew. It is not let off the hook by the notoriously tough Zen masters until it is finally forced to give up and, for once, shut up. Having experienced this first 'satori', this taste of the relief and peace of 'no-mind' and the accompanying immediacy of experience of the real world that is now possible, the meditator, when the mind recovers from its exhaustion, will now have a yardstick by which to compare this direct 'knowing' of the real world with the illusory 'knowing about' that the mind trades in. The mind is, in fact, like a second-hand dealer, continually trying to sell us junk. We are his best customers because we are unaware and suckers for lines like: 'This will make you happy' or 'This is really you'.

The koan 'Who am I?' is doubly useful: hidden within this seemingly innocent inquiry is a fathomless ocean in which the monkey-mind will eventually sink without trace. In the process it will have waded more or less confidently through the shallows of socially-bestowed identity and status, floundered in conditioned ego-roles and self-images and eventually drowned in philosophical and religious speculation. For there is no intellectual answer to this question: my 'suchness' is a pre-verbal experience of myself that is of its nature undefinable.

The greatest boon offered by meditation is getting the difference between descriptions and intellectual understanding and wordless experiencing with the body and the senses — literally, in Fritz Perls' words, 'losing your mind and coming to your senses'. The koan 'Who am I?' is also a reminder not to identify with whatever may be plaguing you right now.

TRATAK (GAZING)

Another device to still the mind so that we can experience directly is 'gazing'. The object of our gazing is not really important, provided it is not ugly or otherwise disturbing. Traditionally it can be at the flame of a lighted candle, a flower, a religious image or the picture of a guru. The point is that not moving the eyes restricts input of information for the brain to process and thus does not give the mind much scope to air its opinions, projections, likes and dislikes about virtually everything it sees.

There is a limit to what views the mind can have on a rose, or a candle flame. When it tries to think about something else, keep bringing your attention back to the object of your contemplation. Remember you are not trying to hallucinate but simply to see what is there, or really, more to *feel* this rose, this flame, this beloved Master. Don't glare; relax and enjoy what you are looking at, keeping eyes soft and unfocused.

LISTENING

Just listening is the quickest way I know to bring me out of my mind, my private world, into the present, the real world. Meditation is about relaxing and non-doing, being open, receptive, impartial — like the ears. You may hear but you cannot listen when you are thinking; the noise in your head blots out sound from the objective world. Then, in fact, you are choosing to listen to the disjointed and repetitive ramblings inside your head rather than to the kaleidoscope of sounds outside you. If we externalized this constant internal talking to ourselves we would probably be certified by alarmed relatives who are unaware that they are in the same boat.

Meditation centers your awareness and for this listening is ideal. All that is required for listening is your awareness, i.e. you, minus your stuff — opinions, judgements and so on. What you choose to give your attention to is less important than giving yourself this experience of emptiness. clarity and receptivity. Listen to music without evaluating it as good or bad, allowing the composer to express himself as he feels. Be aware of, but don't identify with, any concepts or feelings stimulated by the music. 'Spacing out' can be nice but it is not meditation.

Listen to your environment in the same way, as if the various sounds, for example, traffic, were being made by different instruments in an orchestra. Some schools of meditation (for example, TM) employ internal listening to a mantra as a device for quieting the mind.

SLOWING DOWN

Meditation is to relax into your own being, to 'come home' to your most intimate self, after being caught up with what's going on in the world. It is very much about slowing down and 'switching off' and the following may make this easier.

* preliminary unwinding by doing a few of the stretching and body awareness exercises described in chapter four.
* meditating by candlelight or with lights turned down low.
* putting on soft, soothing music as a background. 'New Age' or suitably evocative instrumental music would do, or a tape of sounds from Nature like ocean waves or birdsong. The latter can be bought from certain record dealers.
* meditating regularly at the same time and in the same room makes it easier to slip into the meditative space.
* becoming aware of your breathing and counting from one to ten after each exhalation. After counting ten exhalations do another set of ten and by then your mind should have quietened down sufficiently for you just to sit.
* repeating silently a soothing mantra like 'relax', 'relax' or any similarly calming word. Feel that you are sinking down as you repeat the mantra.
* let your attention centre on the hara and the lower part of your body.

Do not meditate after meals, taking drugs or stimulants, or before retiring for the night. Either you will be too sleepy to meditate or meditating will make you too alert to sleep.

MEDITATION AND HEALING

Meditating regularly will not only relax you and make you easier to be with, more tolerant, less serious or easily ruffled. It harmonises body and mind, calms the emotions and re-opens communication with the deeper levels of the psyche wherein reside our innate wisdom, intuition and the capacity to heal ourselves. Whenever we slip into the alpha state of 'conscious sleep' in deep meditation we are, paradoxically, both at our most vulnerable and our most powerful. At such times we are as open as we will ever be to receiving insights and inspiration in handling any problems we may be experiencing in our lives. Also, from this clear and one-pointed space, any visualisations or affirmations we choose to make will be particularly powerful in effect. If we or our loved ones are sick, picture whoever is ill surrounded by gold light and being restored to radiant health. Beam out loving energy to family or friends who are absent or in danger and surround them with a golden circle to protect them from harm. Make affirmations to cancel out any negative self-image that causes you pain and to empower you to be any way you would like to be.

After meditating, try to avoid losing energy by rushing, talking and doing too much too soon.

DANCING

Dancing, like any exercise, can be meditation. By itself it is perhaps *the* perfect meditation technique. It demands relaxed alertness, listening to the music and present-centeredness; it is non-serious, non-goal-orientated. It gets you grounded, centered in your body not your mind, and high. But for dancing to be a meditation it has to be more than just a mechanical shuffle round the floor (with, perhaps, an eye on the available 'talent') or the cool 'how am I doing' disco style.

For dancing to be meditative it has to be whole-hearted, surrendering the body to the rhythm of the music and allowing it to move in the way most natural to it. Flowing with the music, celebrating this moment totally and enjoying a respite from your worries and preoccupations — this is what meditation is all about.

MEDITATION IN ACTION

What has been said of dancing is true of every activity in which we are likely to be engaged. Everything can become a meditation, including the most ordinary everyday chores like doing the washing-up or going to the toilet. As with dancing and sitting, what transforms mere activity into meditative action is awareness and wholeheartedness.

'Everything is zazen,' said Suzuki Roshi, a Zen monk who first taught me sitting meditation. Observing him during 'sesshins' — concentrated periods of zazen extending over several days — I saw what he meant. To everything he did, from ringing the bell between sessions to eating his food during breaks, he brought the same awareness and composure as when sitting in zazen. There is a Zen saying: 'Walk or sit, but don't wobble,' roughly rendered also by the old song lyric: 'It ain't what you do, it's the way that you do it.'

The application of this Zen exhortation of giving undivided attention to and really feeling what you are doing, is exemplified, for example, in the tea ceremony or in 'ikebana', the art of flower-arranging. Being really *present* in whatever you are doing imparts to you an unmistakable grace, effortlessness and enjoyment in the 'little things'. Simplicity, ease, naturalness, spontaneity — the 'zen of feeling good' — is about being childlike yet not childish.

But before we can attain this effortlessness, this relaxation into whatever we are doing, we must first become aware that we are doing it at all. In the course of the day keep waking yourself up from the sleep that we call random thinking and robot-like activity by remembering what you are doing. For example, when walking down the street, really experience what this particular walk is like, fresh, new, unlike any other you have taken in your life or will ever take again.

Your mind will want to leap ahead and fantasize about what it will be like when you reach your destination or come up with anything else to stop you enjoying what is happening right *now*. Say to yourself something like 'Now I am walking' or simply 'walking, walking', and feel what it is really like to be walking at all, here and now, down this particular street. The more you learn to come out of the past and future, which is mind, into the present, which is life, the more you will feel you are really living.

POSTSCRIPT

In conclusion, here are my two favourite Zen stories.

No. 1

A famous samurai travelled for days to a remote monastery to see a Zen Master. When he was brought into the Master's presence he bowed and asked: 'Wise one, tell me: what is heaven and what is hell?' The Master, not even looking up, answered with a contemptuous snort: 'Why should I? You are such a stupid asshole you couldn't even begin to understand!' Zen Masters were notorious for their plain speaking but this was too much for the samurai. Furious, he drew his sword and held it over the Master's head. 'I'll kill you for that,' he shouted, his face contorted with rage. The Master now looked at him for the first time and said in a gentle voice: 'Now you are in hell.' The samurai understood immediately. Casting away his sword he knelt, all anger gone, to touch the Master's feet in gratitude. When he finally looked up at the Master the latter smiled and told him: 'Now you are in heaven.'

No. 2: Present-centeredness

A Zen monk became aware, while walking through a forest, that he was being stalked by a tiger. Terrified, he began to run but when he looked over his shoulder he could see the big cat gaining on him. Suddenly he found himself at the edge of a cliff and, desperate, leaped off the edge. Fortunately, as he fell, his robe became hooked on a branch growing out of the side of the cliff. As he hung thus, suspended in mid-air, he could hear the tiger growling above him, while below him, too (horror of horrors!), another tiger was pacing up and down, lashing its tail and licking its jaws in anticipation.

Just then the poor monk felt the branch from which he was hanging starting to shake. A large rat had emerged from a hole in the cliff-face and was busily gnawing its way through the narrow branch. What to do? The monk resigned himself to the certain death awaiting him below when the branch should finally give way. At that moment he suddenly spied a cluster of strawberries within arm's length of him. He reached out, picked one and ate it. No strawberry before had ever tasted to him as truly delicious as this one.

The tigers and the strawberries are always there — it is your choice which you give your attention to.

FURTHER READING

Readers interested in exploring further any of the self-help approaches we have been discussing should find the following book list useful. All titles are recently-published paperbacks, readable and readily available in most bookshops.

Doreen E. Bayly, *Reflexology Today* (Thorsons, 1985)

M. Blate, *How to Heal Yourself Using Foot Acupressure* (Routledge & Kegan Paul, 1983)

The Natural Healer's Acupressure Handbook (Routledge & Kegan Paul, 1980)

M. Blate with G.C. Watson, *How to Relieve Arthritis* (Arkana, 1985)

Patricia Byrivers, *Goodbye to Arthritis* (Century Arrow, 1985)

Moira Carpenter, *Curing PMT the Drug-Free Way* (Century Arrow, 1986)

Anne Clark, *What Can I Eat! (Allergy Free Cooking)* (Angus & Robertson, 1986)

The Pocket Fibre Counter (Muller, 1982)

Adelle Davis, *Let's Eat Right and Keep Fit* (Unwin, 1985)

Let's Get Well (Unwin, 1985)

Alec Forbes, *The Bristol Diet* (Century Arrow, 1986)

Richard Grossman, *The Other Medicines* (Pan, 1986)

Maurice Hanssen, *E for Additives* (Thorsons, 1986)

Liz Hodgkinson, *Addictions* (Thorsons, 1986)

Patrick Holford, *The Whole Health Manual* (Thorsons, 1984)

Sandra Horn, *Relaxation* (Thorsons, 1986)

B.K.S. Iyengar, *The Concise Light on Yoga* (Unwin, 1985)

A. Kaye and D.C. Matchan, *Reflexology* (Thorsons, 1986)

Leslie Kenton, *10 Day Clean-Up Plan* (Century, 1986)

Brenda Kidman, *A Gentle Way With Cancer* (Century Arrow, 1986)

L. LeShan, *How to Meditate* (Turnstone, 1983)

Sampson Lipton, *Conquering Pain* (Dunitz, 1984)

Richard Mackarness, *Not All in the Mind* (Pan, 1976)

Jane Madders, *Stress and Relaxation* (Dunitz, 1982)

Marshall Mandell, *Lifetime Arthritis Relief System* (Century Arrow, 1984)

Janette Marshall *High-Fibre Cooking* (Thorsons, 1984)

Leonard Mervyn *Complete Guide to Vitamins and Minerals* (Thorsons, 1986)

S. Matthews-Simonton, O.C. Simonton, J.L. Creighton, *Getting Well Again* (Bantam, 1978)

Alice Neville, *Who's Afraid of Agoraphobia* (Century Arrow, 1986)

I. Oswald and K. Adam, *Get A Better Night's Sleep* (Dunitz, 1981)

Barbara Paterson, *The Allergy Connection* (Thorsons, 1985)

Connie Peck, *Controlling Chronic Pain* (Fontana, 1982)

Louis Proto *How to Beat Fatigue* (Century Arrow, 1986)

Alan Stoddard, *The Back — Relief From Pain* (Dunitz, 1979)

M. Struna and C. Church, *Self Massage* (Hutchinson, 1984)

Maxine Tobias and Mary Stewart, *Stretch and Relax* (Dorling Kindersley, 1985)

A. Wallace and B. Henkin, *The Psychic Healing Book* (Turnstone, 1981)

Betty Wood, *The Healing Power of Colour* (Aquarian, 1984)

S. Yesudian and E. Haitch, *Yoga and Health* (Unwin, 1986)

Dahong Zhuo, *The Chinese Exercise Book* (Thorsons, 1986)

INDEX